et

veritas

Brescia College Library

London   -   Ontario

PQ2323

.L8Z55

WRITERS AND CRITICS

Chief Editor

A. NORMAN JEFFARES

Advisory Editors

DAVID DAICHES

C. P. SNOW

For many years Jules Laforgue was regarded as a typical nineteenth-century decadent. His refusal to come to terms with the world as it is was dismissed as adolescent, and his poems were regarded as wilfully affected attempts to be original at any cost. Pound, however, described him as "the most sophisticated of all French poets," not only because he recognised the essential modernity of Laforgue's sceptical outsider's view of the world, but also because—in his free-verse poems—Laforgue succeeded in fashioning a poetic idiom that would express the new sensibility. It was his achievement in both these matters that was noted by T. S. Eliot at the beginning of the century.

In this book, Mr Collie has attempted to show that behind the conventional *fin-de-siècle* pose there was a serious poet, whose writings show a consistent artistic purpose and whose last poems completely justify the influence he has had in the twentieth century.

Since leaving Cambridge in 1957, Mr Collie has lived in various parts of Canada, and is at present Assistant Professor in the Department of English at Mount Allison University. He is at work on a critical introduction to modern French poetry.

LAFORGUE

MICHAEL COLLIE

OLIVER AND BOYD
EDINBURGH AND LONDON

OLIVER AND BOYD LTD
Tweeddale Court
Edinburgh 1

39A Welbeck Street
London, W. 1

First published 1963

Printed in Great Britain for Oliver and Boyd Ltd
by Robert MacLehose and Co. Ltd, Glasgow

CONTENTS

ABBREVIATED TITLES USED IN THE TEXT

O.C.	=	*Oeuvres complètes de Jules Laforgue* (Mercure de France 1920–30).
M.P.	=	*Mélanges posthumes.*
E.C.	=	Edition de la Connaissance.
M.L.	=	*Moralités légendaires.*
L.A.	=	*Lettres à un ami.*

CHAPTER I

THE MAKINGS OF A NIHILIST

There is a poetry which derives from the tension that is felt between man as a social being and man as a thinking individual, as though the two were inherently irreconcilable. This is a traditional theme. But in the latter part of the nineteenth century it assumed a new importance because by that time to define the position of the individual in the world at large was no longer a peripheral problem concerning only the abnormal or the eccentric, but one which was crucial to anyone who thought at all irrespective of whether his subsequent reflexion led him to orthodoxy or dissent. Nevertheless, Jules Laforgue has been known as a dilettante and a decadent; a dilettante because he preferred a downright evident pose to an anonymous conformity which accepted life as it was, and a decadent because in rejecting normality he undermined, or tended to undermine, accepted values and conventional practices. Yet this kind of assessment is not quite good enough, for several reasons. The first is that the theme which informs a great number of Laforgue's poems—How can the thinking, sensitive individual consciousness be reconciled to a world which seems alien to it?—is no longer merely the concern of decadents, but is now, for better or worse, a matter of central and unavoidable importance, at least in literature and art. The second is that emphasis on the frivolous, dilettante poems, entertaining as many of them are, has tended to distract attention both from Laforgue's best and later poems, and from the conscious development and experimentation which led to them. The third reason is that the kind of poem which Laforgue wrote, though it may have appeared eccentric, obscure, or meretricious at the time, has now been absorbed into the living literature both of France and of England, so that, looking back, one is impressed by the technical inventiveness which enabled Laforgue to find a way of expressing an essentially "modern" attitude of mind. Most important of all, there are good poems which have often been neglected by critics anxious to decide such questions as whether or not Laforgue was a Symbolist.

Beneath the labels, then, of "dilettante" and "decadent," there is a core of feeling which informed the majority of Laforgue's poems. For Laforgue, as for many others, it was an ambiguous feeling: on the one side, a miserable, adolescent sense of inferiority and incompatibility; on the other, an assurance of superiority amounting almost to arrogance. So the poet wanders through the city street, looks in at the warmly lighted *bourgeois* homes, and feels a complete loneliness, isolation and lack of love. On the other hand, in another mood, people engaged in that other, "exterior" life are unthinking fools, automata, animals to be regarded with utter disdain. As it appears to the reader, though it would be different and more complex for the poet himself, Laforgue's dissatisfaction is both social and intellectual. The habits associated with life in society, its institutions, premises and traditions, seem to the poet to lack ultimate sanction; he therefore rejects them as having no bearing on his own, personal life. He rejects normality as such, not merely the particular social conditions in France at the time, though these were bad enough to justify the attitude. Again, the desire for a feeling of intellectual certainty, at the centre of European life and art since the seventeenth century at least, as it became less likely to be satisfied became also more important, so that as other "certainties" were one by one destroyed the mind craved for greater assurances than it could tell itself it was reasonable to expect. This was the root cause of the nihilistic attitude.

These various considerations are not mentioned here because they were such an important part of contemporary thinking both in France and in England, and were therefore the background against which Laforgue wrote. The intellectual dilemmas of that period are too well known to require discussion here. They are mentioned because they were Laforgue's explicit concern and starting point. They were not, because of this, the subject of his poems, except perhaps for a few of the earliest, but gave rise to the feelings which informed the poems whatever their subject. These feelings might be expressed as scepticism, or as a morbid distaste for the physical world, or as intellectual frustration, or as a personal sense of failure and emptiness. Similarly the same feeling will be expressed in one poem with deep irony, but in another as an austere withdrawal from or renunciation of worldly things. (In the poetry of Laforgue, as in that of Eliot, irony and renunciation derive from the same point.) Whatever the case, the layers of irony and sentiment and attitude tend to conceal the poet's real concern, as does his dilettante pose in actual life, so that the majority of his poems, certainly until the last year of his life, are in the minor key. Consequently, a reader's attitude to Laforgue will be at first determined by how seriously he takes these primary underlying concerns of the poet. If he feels that it is impossible for any one man to achieve a satisfactory synthesis of experience, and that to desire it is only a sign of immaturity, he will find it hard to sympathise with the poet who refuses to accept the various aspects of existence as fundamentally incompatible and mysterious, and who in fact prefers almost any pose, however artificial, to a placid acceptance of things as they are. If, on the other hand, the reader feels that the need for understanding and coherence, without perjuring the sensibility, is of prime

importance, he will not be unmoved by Laforgue's
ironical view of things, and indeed will be free to make
the most of the poems themselves.

At this point, then, one is only marking a difference,
the difference between 1963 and 1880. The compromise
which Laforgue refused to accept is now, in the twentieth
century, much more of a fact of existence, so that a man
in his position would not now have to react against
orthodoxy, or against *bourgeois* conformity and hypo-
crisy as he did, but rather against the suave urbanity that
affects to know that there are no answers to fundamental
questions, and that the only approach to an ethical
attitude now possible is a sophisticated pragmatism. It
was Laforgue's refusal or inability to make this kind of
compromise that led him to the extremist attitudes of
"nihilism" and "decadence." He refused to come to
terms with "normal life," and refused to abandon his
own thoughts and intuitions for the sake of a comfortable
conformity. He recognised the weakness of this position,
of his "useless, adolescent heart,"[1] and it is on this recog-
nition that the irony of all his work depends. But since,
like Hardy, he found no intellectual answer to the determinism within which his mind was trapped, he preferred
the pose of the dilettante and the renunciation of the
dandy to any compromise with a life which was obviously
unsatisfactory and sordid. In this way he identifies himself with Hamlet, for example, since Hamlet advises
Ophelia, whom he loved, not to accommodate herself to
life. If these generalisations have any truth in them, one
could say that the inadequacy of Laforgue's life was far
more of a disaster than it might seem to be now, and
that his move to art as a compensation for the futility of
actual existence is only disingenuous in retrospect, having
at that time the force of necessity that circumstance
seems always to impose.

The circumstances of Laforgue's life made him a dilettante, and during the process he learnt to be a poet. This

process has three stages. He was first the youthful cynic, depressed by thought; then the blasé dilettante, finding the consolation in art which he could not find in life; then the poet, passing beyond theory at the moment that he found a way of giving his view of himself and his world imaginative substance.

"Then I think, and, after having thought, I doubt. I doubt if our thought rhymes with anything real in the universe. And I'm bored: and, as M. Bourget says, I chew at the bitter foliage of spleen."[2] This is the first step, the intense, often adolescent, brooding speculation of his early years in Paris and the first few months in Germany. After that, there is a new kind of leisure, and the cultivation of pose, the attempt at a mask, the make-believe of a Pierrot, and the half-seriousness of the aesthete. "As for myself, I lead as always the life of a dilettante," he writes to the blue-stocking Mme Mültzer, in 1882:

> Know, dear poet, that before having literary ambitions, I had the enthusiasms of a prophet, and that for a while I used to dream each night of consoling Savanarola in his prison. Now, I am a dilettante in everything, with from time to time bouts of universal spleen. I watch the Carnival of life passing by: policemen, artists, sovereigns, ministers, lovers, etc. I smoke blonde cigarettes, I write poetry and prose, perhaps also do a little etching, and I await death.[3]

His symbol is a passive one, Watteau's painting of Gilles in the Louvre; and his occupation, though in these years (1882–85) it is a strain to use the word, is art. Finally, in the last year and a half of his life, there is a sudden burst of activity; three volumes of poems are written; he brings to an end his years of pose and boredom by leaving Germany; and from another point of view, he finds in the last of his poems an art form which contains and realises his particular consciousness, to the extent that a few weeks before his death he abandons his usual reticence in a letter to his sister:

> It's a long time since you have known anything of my literary life. It would be too long to tell you in detail, but know, in a word, that I have the right to be proud: there is not a writer of my generation to whom a better future is promised.[4]

Laforgue would not boast except to give consolation to his sister, as will be seen, but the letter does seem to indicate a sense of certainty as a poet which has made the former posing unnecessary.

The last poems, published posthumously in 1890 by Dujardin and Fenéon, are themselves sufficient justification for any interest in Laforgue's life as a whole. The writing of any particular, preliminary poem, taken by itself, may not appear to have the urgency necessary for good poetry, but not only does the poet's development become intelligible when, in retrospect, it can be regarded as a whole, but also the force of the *Derniers Vers* themselves is made more clear by some knowledge of what was important to Laforgue in the earlier stages. This book is written on the assumption that the *Derniers Vers* represent Laforgue's most mature and accomplished work, and that something is to be gained by discussing the poems as a volume, rather than as posthumous fragments. There are, however, other considerations. Firstly, there is no complete edition of Laforgue's work, not even a competent selection, either in French or English. There is thus more cause than in other cases for attempting to view the work as a whole and make some sense out of the apparent chaos. One of Laforgue's first editors, Fenéon, a well known anarchist, was arrested by police who, at that critical moment, thought the poet's papers were coded documents. Though this might be thought bad enough, it was not such a disaster as the work of subsequent editors, who not only re-arranged and in one case "gently rewrote" the papers that they had obtained by chance, but also, by keeping the manuscripts to themselves, succeeded in creating a closed shop, so that at the moment there is no sure way of correcting the innumerable errors in the printed text. (A student willing to be frustrated by this might begin by reading the account of manuscripts in the 1954 edition of *Moralités légendaires*.) Secondly, in England and North America, Laforgue has been known chiefly because of T. S. Eliot's interest in him. Though this is greater than may have been thought, (greater anyway than Eliot acknowledged in his Preface to Pound's poems), the legitimate focus on the major poet necessarily distracts one's attention from the nonetheless genuine merits of his predecessor. Eliot's reading of the three volume edition of Laforgue, which he obtained in Boston, probably in 1911 when he returned to the United States, was of course completely thorough: a comparison of these volumes with Eliot's early work reveals innumerable parallels. More important, it must have been that Eliot's summer reading was one of the ways by which he came to form his own thoughts on symbol, metre, free-verse, and the kind of poem that might express an intense personal intuition of the world without sentimentality. Eliot learnt from Laforgue; later English poets learnt from Eliot. Nevertheless, one might more easily understand the appeal that Laforgue had for Eliot by attempting first to understand him in his own terms. Thirdly, Laforgue stands at a point which is particularly interesting for anyone concerned with twentieth century poetry, whether in France or England. He marks the change from poetry as communication to poetry as art; he represents, at an early stage, the "new" sensibility—acute, dissatisfied, at odds with the world; and, like Hardy, Swinburne, Hopkins, and others in England, he uses a new freedom to experiment in the craft of poetry, eventually creating a new idiom and a new form.

Laforgue partly satisfies romantic expectations about
the life of a poet: a remote birth, a life in exile, and a
tubercular death. Born in Montevideo in 1860, his only
recorded early memory was the sixty-five days boredom
of a traumatic voyage across the Atlantic when the
family returned to France six years later. An unhappy
but apparently uneventful childhood was brought to an
end by the family's move from Tarbes to Paris, by his
triple failure at the Baccalaureat, by his mother's death
in 1877, and his father's in 1881, and by two years solitary
loafing on the banks of the Seine and in the Bibliothèque
Nationale. It is true that, during these years, he made
three friends, Bourget, Henry and Kahn, whom he was
to know until his death and who, one by one, played an
important part in shaping his life. It is true also that he
had in the end a stroke of luck which relieved his boredom
and in another way directed his interests: for the last
few months of his time in Paris he worked part-time as
assistant to Ephrussi, the art dealer and critic. But he
did not enjoy the actual company of these new friends
for very long. In November 1881, on the recommenda-
tion of Bourget and Ephrussi, he was appointed French
reader to the Empress Augusta of Germany, and, joining
the German Court on 30 Nov. at Coblentz, he immediately began the twice-daily readings which were to make
the pattern of his existence for the next five years. One
form of essential loneliness was thus exhanged for another.
The five years of Court routine, which, with mechanical
regularity, were punctuated by moves from Berlin to the
royal residences at Baden-Baden, Coblentz and Potsdam,
were not interrupted by anything in the nature of an
event, and were only relieved by Laforgue's greater dis-
like of Baden-Baden, and in later years by an occasional
holiday. Laforgue appeared to the world, according to
Wyzewa, one of his later editors, as a correctly dressed
curate, prim, black-suited, and with top-hat and cane;
to his acquaintances, like Bernstein or Lindenlaub, as an

art critic, a connoisseur, a dandy; and to his friends, as a confirmed but amiable cynic, who wrote unreserved, unaffected, genuine letters, but who never quite told them everything and who never quite satisfied their expectations. In 1886, after achieving a small measure of success with the publication of *Les Complaintes* and *L'Imitation de Notre Dame la Lune*, or at least a measure of personal satisfaction, and therefore confidence, he decided to return to Paris. Perhaps this was the only decision he ever made. He was helped towards it by the fact that, having previously declared that there were three species—men, women, and Englishwomen—he had that autumn become engaged to Leah Lee, who was one of the last group. He left Germany in September 1886, was married in England on the last day of December, and moved to Paris (8 rue de Commaille) in January, with no money, with no immediate prospect of an income, and with little idea of what to do except hope for a quick publication of his book on Germany. By this time, however, he was too ill to work, and he died a few months later, of tuberculosis, or of the incidental pneumonia, in August 1887.

This brief account of Laforgue's life is not a summary. In the large company of *fin-de-siècle* decadents, he had little difficulty in cultivating the appropriate air of *ennui*: he was genuinely bored. Literally nothing ever happened, either in his life, or in the life of the Court. A man's life, however, does not consist of events alone. It was during these same years that Laforgue wrote his first volume of poems, *Le Sanglot de la terre*. In Germany he became knowledgeable in contemporary art. And at the same time his thinking about poetry gradually developed and matured. As has been suggested already, this development, the very basis of the mature writing in the last year of his life, can be seen and followed in a number of ways. On the one hand, the poems themselves, *Le Sanglot de la terre*, express more vividly than anything that might be said what Laforgue's early life was like, while

B

the difference between them and the next volume, *Les Complaintes*, makes his technical accomplishment very clear, whatever a reader might think of the poems themselves. On the other hand, the same development can be seen easily enough in such prose as has been published: in the two volumes of letters, published as Volumes IV and V of the so-called *Oeuvres complètes*; in the letters to Gustave Kahn, which, as *Lettres à un ami*, were published by Mercure de France in 1941 and which have a far greater intrinsic interest than the others; and in the various fragments and notes as they were once published in *Mélanges posthumes*.

A few of these accounts refer to Laforgue's very early days in Paris, when his family, except for his brother Emile, had returned to Tarbes, and when he lived alone in rue Monsieur le Prince. There is a letter to his sister written in September 1881, which describes his initial loneliness in such a wistful and melancholy way that the embarrassments of his solitary life are played down, and the seriousness of his attitude to life disguised. But later he refers to these same few weeks in a different manner:

> Only two or three people know anything of the life I lived in Paris, two years ago. And yet, really, only I myself know.—When I read through my diary of that period, I shudder to think why I did not die of it.[5]

In the same way, the little novel *Stéphane Vassiliew*, which was recovered by Ruchon a few years ago and which describes the loneliness, suffering and frustration of a boy at school, is probably of the same date and may very well be autobiographical, for it is hard to consider a piece as intense as this to be anything else. "And Stephen was living, for his part, in the endless torture of his inward existence, of memories which were his although he did not know them."[6] And later: "His life was nothing more than a succession of worries that he did not understand. Throughout the whole world there was no one who loved him."[7] Yet again, in *Mélanges posthumes*, there are papers which must refer to 1880 or 1881:

Two years of solitude in libraries, without love, without friends, but with the fear of death. And nights of meditation in the atmosphere of Sinai.

Then a novel. . . . It is the autobiography of my organism, of my thought, expressed through a painter as a life, as the ambitions of a painter, but a thoughtful painter, a pessimistic and macabre Chenevard.[8]

In a way which characterises the poor editing of Laforgue's work, the other version of these papers, Volume II. of the Connaissance edition, does not include the above passage: but it does contain notes of similar tone, with the same youthful, undeveloped concern and urgency. For example:

The fury of wishing to know oneself—of plunging beneath one's conscious culture towards the African interior of our unconscious domain.

I feel myself so poor, so naked as I see myself, Laforgue, in relation to the outside world. And I have rich mines, veins, underwater worlds which ferment unknown. Ah! it is there that I would like to live, it's there that I would die. With strange flowers turning on their stems like the wax heads of the hair stylists, with magical settings of stones, as where the Galatée of Moreau sleeps and is watched by Polyphème. . . .[9]

These passages indicate Laforgue's state of mind while he was writing his first poems. The intensity, the lack of love, and the fear of death, associate themselves inevitably with the fatalism which results from abstract thought, where the thought lacks any kind of orientation and the abstraction occurs on a level remote from the actual experience that might inform it. A man in this position, whether physically isolated or not, is obliged to depend upon the one thing he has—his own thinking. But it is irremediably introspective: he thinks about thought. In Laforgue's case, since he saw the irony of this predicament, and since indeed it was just this ironical appreciation that led him to cultivate the attitudes of a dandy, the only rational view of life that seemed possible was a frankly resigned and relativist one. This he adopted, both in life, and in art. His writing from beginning to end is studded with this strain of acceptance—"More than ever I'm the slave of destiny," and "I believe that everything is written, that everything is marked out in advance."[10] Though the opposite is as often true, it would be rather too glib to write off Laforgue's concern as merely adolescent or exaggerated, not only because it was genuine, but also because it was by no means exceptional, but representative of the times and standing in need of an answer. A philosophy would be much more glib if it did not provide a satisfactory route past this particular *impasse*. In art, Laforgue's formative experiences were his attendance at Taine's lectures on painting, and his work, for a few months later in 1881, as assistant to Charles Ephrussi. The first was a point of departure: from that time onwards he was uncompromisingly opposed to any idea of art which depended on the notion of Ideal beauty or which ascribed moral values to painting or sculpture. Indeed he was opposed to any form of aesthetic dogmatism. The second gave him a grounding in critical method and introduced him at first hand to the works of Impressionist painters, many of whose canvases were on the walls of the room in which he worked.

Laforgue was a child of his time, but the birth carried with it no explicit or satisfactory explanation. To speculate about the origins of that *fin-de-siècle*, decadent or nihilistic attitude which characterised the period, and of which he later turned out to be a complete exponent, wherever the emphasis be placed (whether on the low morale of France after its earlier upheavals, or the social

disintegration and change prevalent throughout Europe,
or the clash between science and orthodoxy) seems not
to explain his particular predicament, which he arrived
at by a private approach, without reference to any
leader or guide. He permitted circumstance to make
him what he was. Before he left Paris, however, he had
made three friends, more or less compatible in tempera-
ment, who not only kept him mentally alive in Germany,
but also helped him materially at various stages of his
career. The first was Gustave Kahn, whom Laforgue
met at the "Club des Hydropathes." Kahn later records
his surprise that Laforgue joined the group, which met
at a café, merely to hear poetry read and discussed, and
the *Lettres à un ami* testify to the importance of the friendship from Laforgue's point of view. Probably Laforgue
had never spoken freely about poetry before. A few
years later Kahn founded, directed, and edited the
magazine *La Vogue* in which Laforgue published his
most important work. Kahn also introduced Laforgue
to Charles Henry, another unreligious intellectual with a
lively mind and wide interests, a mathematician who
dabbled in literature and art, and who was shortly to
become a librarian at the Sorbonne. He was only slightly
older than Laforgue and gave him the same kind of equal
companionship, a friendship which lasted through the
early years in Germany, until he personally had seen
Laforgue's first published volume, *Les Complaintes*,
through the press. Thirdly, there was Paul Bourget, who,
when Laforgue first met him, had published his first two
books, *La Vie inquiète* and *Edel*. It was he who introduced
Laforgue to Shelley and Tennyson, and more immediately important, discussed and criticised his poems.
Bourget declined to publish the letters he had received
from Laforgue, but one can gather something of the importance of their early friendship from the way in which
Laforgue wrote to his brother, Emile, as late as July
1886:

I remember the time when I would take Bourget plays, chapters of a novel, and masses of verse, thinking to myself: This will stagger him! And the following Sunday he would reply: 'You do not yet know the French language, or the poet's craft, and you are still not thinking for yourself.'[11]

—advice which Laforgue had followed by suppressing his first poems, (*Le Sanglot de la terre*), by spending his years in Germany experimenting on metre, (*Les Complaintes*), and by searching out at last an original synthesis of subject and form (*Derniers Vers*).

This group of friends came together at a time which was crucial to all of them. They shared their ideas and interests, then developed independently from the common starting point. In Laforgue's case, the first step was the writing of *Le Sanglot de la terre*, a collection of poems written for the most part in Paris but later suppressed as being too rhetorical and derivative. The general intention of this first volume is given in *Mélanges posthumes* in a passage which has already been referred to:

MY BOOKS.—A work of literature and a work of prophecy for the modern age.

A volume of poems that I call philosophical. I used to believe naively, without pretentiousness. Then, a sharp break. Two years of solitude in libraries, without friends, without love, but with the fear of death. Nights of meditation in the atmosphere of Sinai. Then I am astonished that philosophers who daily execute the idea of justice, and the idols of religion, metaphysics, and morality, are so little moved, to think that they are not convinced of the existence of these things. Then, astonishment that in our generation there are so few poets who have written a book of this kind. Leconte de Lisle not human enough, too refined in the bourgeois sense, Cazalis too much of a dilettante, Mme Ackermann not accomplished enough,

Sully-Prudhomme too cold, too mechanical, and others with only occasional writings. So I make this book naively—in five parts—Lamma sabacktani, Angoisses, Les poèmes de la Mort, Les poèmes du spleen, Resignation: the story, the diary of a Parisian in 1880, who suffers, doubts, and arrives at Nothingness, against a Parisian background, the sunsets, the Seine, the showers, the wide pavements, the Jablochkoffs, and in the language of the artist, profound and modern, without any care for codes of taste, without fear of shocking, of exaggeration and extravagance, of the grotesque, etc....

This book will be called: *Le Sanglot de la terre*. First part: this will be the lament of thought, of the brain, of the conscience of the earth. A second volume, in which I shall concentrate the whole misery, all the filth of the planet within the innocence of the skies, the baccanalia of history, the splendours of the soul, the Paris barrel-organs, the carnival, the Olympia, the Morgue, the Dupuytren museum, the hospital, love, alcohol: spleen, massacres, the Thebaides, folly, the Salpêtrière.[12]

Though Laforgue does not keep to this scheme, the poems are consistent with it in tone and style. In fact they are too close to the theoretical considerations which are its core. Despite the experimental nature of a few of the poems, the majority have to be regarded as thought versified. As Laforgue is at the stage of supposing that what one thinks is what one is obliged to think, and therefore does not conceal the agony which results from his first look at the world, a poem that ought perhaps to be an interior monologue is made a public statement. "When I organise a descent into myself,"[13] said Laforgue in one of the best of his later poems: *Le Sanglot de la terre* is a preliminary statement from the interior. The world of these poems is an evolutionary, accidental, godless world, in which he is plagued by a desire to know, without ever feeling that ultimate knowledge is possible. "And still wild with anguish and doubt I go on questioning! It is an Enigma at least!"[14] The effect that this enigma has on him he expresses strongly in a number of poems. In "Médiocrité"[15] the world is seen spinning as a mote of dust, a single atom, through an immense universe—"vole avec sa vermine aux vastes profondeurs," Laforgue's bitter view of this coming in the last six lines of the sonnet:

> La plupart vit et meurt sans soupçonner l'histoire
> Du globe, sa misère en l'éternelle gloire,
> Sa future agonie au soleil moribond.
>
> Vertiges d'univers, cieux à jamais en fête!
> Rien, ils n'auront rien su. Combien même s'en vont
> Sans avoir seulement visité leur planète.[16]*

In another evolutionary poem, "Litanies de misère,"[17] he traces the history of the world to the birth of man, who sees "the aimless evil of everything." Laforgue is unable to free himself from the consciousness of this automatic, irresponsible, inexplicable evolutionary progress, or his realisation of how insignificant the individual creature is: not insignificant only, but at best miserable, at the worst vile. The poem ends with lines which describe life after the coming of man:

> La femme hurle aux nuits, se tord et mord ses draps
> Pour pondre des enfants vils, malheureux, ingrats.
>
> La moitié meurt avant un an, dans la misère,
> Sans compter les morts-nés bons à cacher sous terre.
>
> L'homme, les fleurs, les nids, tout sans trêve travaille,
> Car la vie à chaque heure est une âpre bataille.

* Translation of all passages quoted in French will be found among the References at the end of each chapter.

Et malheur aux vaincus, aux faibles, aux trop doux,
Aux trop bons pour vouloir hurler avec les loups.

La faim, l'amour, l'espoir, . . . la maladie,
Puis la mort, c'est toujours la même comédie.

Et d'abord les trois quarts crient: "Pas de quoi manger!"
Et sont pour l'autre quart un perpétuel danger.[18]

These ideas, which lack the acuteness of insight, and which are more like over-obvious marker buoys than the chart of the actual depths which was promised, are expressed more strongly in the more personal poems. Perhaps the slight tension between what he thinks in general and what he feels as a person makes for a better poem. The imagination is still on the loose, but in the personal poems comes closer to actual experience and is therefore to a slight extent more adequately realised. "Pour le livre d'amour"[19] would illustrate this. It begins plaintively and without subtlety: "I could die tomorrow, without ever having loved." And then, as the poem becomes more bitter:

J'ai craché sur l'amour et j'ai tué la chair!
Fou d'orgueil, je me suis roidi contre la vie!
Et seul sur cette Terre à l'Instinct asservie
Je défiais l'Instinct avec un rire amer.

He will have nothing to do with a life of cause and effect, of instinct which is the satisfying of need, of existence *per se*. He will not love to satisfy a need, nor accommodate the flesh merely for comfort, like an organism:

Partout, dans les salons, au théâtre, à l'église,
Devant ces hommes froids, les plus grands, les plus fins,
Et ces femmes aux yeux doux, jaloux ou hautains
Dont on redorerait chastement l'âme exquise.

Je songeais: tous en sont venus là! J'entendais
Les râles de l'immonde accouplement des brutes!

Tant de fanges pour un accès de trois minutes!
Hommes, soyez corrects! ô femmes, minaudez![20]

From this urgent, but rather gross and unimaginative
conception, Laforgue, in the first stage of his development, cultivates a detachment which anticipates the
more sensitive, more controlled irony of the later poems.
The awareness of "our human farce," which is the theme
of *Le Sanglot de la terre*, remains a constant preoccupation
throughout Laforgue's life, and with it the loneliness,
and pride of the romantic, individualistic mind, as
though the very thing "being an individual" involves
this kind of misery. At first the pose which accompanies
this is simple and naive: later it becomes complex. This
volume, for example, is contained by its first poem:

Non, je resterai seul, ici-bas,
Tout à la chère morte phtisique,
Berçant mon coeur trop hypertrophique
Aux éternelles fugues de Bach.[21]

And its last:

Oui, ce monde est bien plat: quant à l'autre, sornettes.
Moi, je vais résigné, sans espoir à mon sort,
Et pour tuer le temps, en attendant la mort,
Je fume au nez des dieux de fines cigarettes.

Allez, vivants, luttez, pauvres futurs squelettes.
Moi, le méandre bleu qui vers le ciel se tord
Me plonge en une extase infinie et m'endort
Comme aux parfums mourants de mille cassolettes.

Et j'entre au paradis, fleuri de rêves clairs
Où l'on voit se mêler en valses fantastiques
Des éléphants en rut à des choeurs de moustiques.

Et puis, quand je m'éveille en songeant à mes vers,
Je contemple, le coeur plein d'une douce joie,
Mon cher pouce rôti comme une cuisse d'oie.[22]

It seems important to give the quality of these poems by quoting one in its entirety. But there are at least two other kinds of poem in this first book which must be referred to briefly. Both anticipate *Les Complaintes* at least in interest if not in achievement, and both may have been written in Berlin rather than in Paris. "Rosace en vitrail"[23] is an attempt to recreate with words the effect of a stained glass window. It is over-worked, and rhetorical, but its intention is artistic rather than philosophical, and therefore points the way to the next stage in Laforgue's career. "La Chanson du petit hyper-trophique"[24] with its oft-quoted refrain—"I hear my beating heart, it is my mother calling me," is a light, colloquial song which anticipates Laforgue's experiments with popular metres and tunes. They are neither of them strong poems, however, and the dominant effect of *Le Sanglot de la terre* as a whole is of a heavy "cosmic" awareness, genuine, but unrelieved by humour or mature insight.

Laforgue went to Germany in 1881. The experience was exactly the same as that known by many Englishmen conscripted during peace-time and sent overseas: an exterior discipline of no evident value, a life of purposeless and often futile activity, hours of boredom, and for a good while a remoteness from local people likely to accentuate any feeling of dissatisfaction or personal uncertainty. When Ephrussi and Bourget together recommended him for the position of French reader at the Court of the Empress Augusta, there was no reason for him to hestitate, and he in fact must have travelled almost immediately to Coblentz, for although his father died at the end of November he did not go to Tarbes for the funeral and indeed was presented to the Empress for the first time on 30 Nov. The new life which started at this point is easy to describe but hard to assess: for five years he occupied a sinecure which enabled him to write. Whether he would still have written without the sinecure, or whether he would have written a different kind of poem, are questions on which one can do no more than speculate. The position was well paid (9000 francs a year) and entailed the minimum of work. Twice a day, for the next five years, usually at 11 a.m. and 7 p.m., he read to the Empress in French, often from the three newspapers he received at her instructions every morning: *L'Indépendance Belge*, *Les Débats*, *and Le Figaro*, and often from popular and acceptable poets like Sully-Prudhomme. The position also gave him a security he had never known before. He prepared his daily readings for a month in advance and at first seldom went out. But he read continuously, began to think of a new kind of poem, worked for an hour a day at his German, corresponded with his Paris friends on art and poetry, and within a year or so was a new man, more relaxed, and with his natural charm no longer inhibited. But he was bored. It is the correspondence that tells us almost everything about Laforgue at this time, for naturally there are few first hand accounts of a man so thoroughly removed from his natural habitat. The letters which have been preserved, however, were written to a small group of correspondents and Laforgue develops a manner of writing which is appropriate, as it were, to his exile and lack of personal contact. In the same way, even those few letters contain surprises. Just as one is beginning to form a coherent picture of the accomplished dandy, for example, one finds that one summer he goes rowing every morning on Lake Lucerne, or throughout the winter skates two hours a day and regrets the first warm days of spring, or explains away his dilatory letter-writing by saying that he has been going to too many balls. One would wish in any case to be quite tentative about a man's life viewed from afar, especially if it is the work rather than the life that is chiefly interesting. Nowadays it is fashionable to believe that there are no secrets, thorough research is on the whole trusted, and, in an atmosphere of general enlightenment, a reader can be tempted into thinking that because he is without inhibitions and knows a great deal he thereby knows everything. But to reveal all that can be revealed is an essentially limited activity in any sphere: with people it is especially limited. In Laforgue's case one can pick out the main threads of his development during the years in Germany, conscious that they represent what it was possible for him to write about, and that other material, such as the unpublished letters to Bourget, might at least modify the overall impression. Three such principal leads take us to his reading, his growing interest in art, and his changing attitude to himself and by implication to his poetry.

Since he was expected to answer to the Empress on anything French he had to be widely read, but it seems likely that without that incentive the long hours of leisure would have confirmed what was already a habit with him. "I am unable to write a line, either of verse or prose," he says, "but I read incessantly."[25] In January he tells Henry:

> The placidity of Berlin exasperates me; I fear it; and I don't write a single line or phrase without wishing to be over-emphatic, to show myself I am free of it. Anyway I have with me my Baudelaire, my Cros, some Stendhal, a pile of Balzac, *En Ménage*, some Taine, and my Hartmann.[26]

This is the same as to say that despite the change in his life he himself is the same. Hartmann's book, *La Philosophie de l'inconscient*, was his temporary Bible. At other places, since he is writing to people who know him well, he only mentions books when there is point, and therefore gives an incomplete picture. He mentions Verlaine, for example, because *Sagesse* is unobtainable in Germany. (Laforgue does not in fact receive a copy until 1883, by which time most of the "Complaintes" have been written.) He knew little Mallarmé, although he had met him once: he knew the *Hérodiade* and the preface to Henry's edition of *Vathek* at this time. As he read *Poètes maudits* in January 1885, he must have known of Rimbaud. He was not, however, greatly affected by him until 1886 when he read *Les Illuminations* in *La Vogue*, that is, before the publication of the *Derniers Vers* but after the writing of all his other work. He acknowledges an affinity with Corbière, but claims (in a letter to Trézenick in August 1885) to have written the bulk of the "Complaintes" six months before the publication of *Les Poètes maudits* and a year before receiving a copy of *Les Amours jaunes*. He refers frequently to Rollinat, Richepin, and Cros, though usually to disassociate himself from what they have done. On the other hand, there are two poets whose work he always respects. He over-emphasises his general indebtedness to Bourget. And he says in a letter to Kahn: "These days my passion for Baudelaire is renewed."[27]

There is disagreement over Laforgue's knowledge of English and German. It seems likely, however, that he achieved a working competence in each. He may have read Hartmann in French, but he certainly read Heine and Schopenhauer in German. Similarly, though he did not know the language in Paris when Bourget began to introduce him to English poets, from Berlin he plagues Henry for the English dictionary he had left behind in France, which he needed then for translating articles in art journals and magazines. He occasionally records the reading of a novel in English, and by 1885 there is no doubt at all that he was reading *Hamlet* in its original form. By and large, though one can list his reading, as he does himself, it remains true that the poems themselves tell one as much about his susceptibilities as his letters. Besides this, where there was a debt he did his best, not to conceal it, but to learn from it and move further in his own work. Both Heine and Baudelaire were congenial to him in this sense, but his desire was for originality at

any cost: he was far too self-conscious and acute to let
pass anything in the slightest way derivative, unless controlled by irony. From yet another point of view, there is
a distinction which remained valid throughout his life:
he was vitally interested in poets, but learnt from
painters.

His sustained interest in art is much more definite.
"You tell me to work. . . . You will see,"[28] he writes to
Ephrussi. Laforgue is toying with a novel at this point
(*Le Raté*), it comes to nothing, his early verse has gone
stale, and it is painting and art in general that he cultivates. "All that I shall be able to do here will be to become a scholar in art,"[29] he writes in a letter to Henry in
December 1881, lamenting the loss of the atmosphere of
Paris and recording his first impression of Germans, who
"are not artists in the complex sense, as with us." In a
letter in the same vein to Ephrussi, a month later: "I read
a page of Spinoza or of Hartmann, and I am above all
this social glitter by a thousand miles. There is nothing
but art."[30] A mere glance at the letters will show how
varied this interest became: it is not necessary to list
here the particular works he discusses or the museums
and exhibitions he visits. It can be said, however, that
beneath his dilettante pose there was genuine knowledge
and genuine concern, and an enthusiasm which had two
important results. The first was that he gained the confidence necessary for his poetry by writing about painting. The second was that in thinking about painting he
not only came to see poetry as art, instead of naive communication, but also learnt how to achieve with words
the same effects as painters were achieving on their
canvases. Kahn, in retrospect, has said that Laforgue's
first published work was on Watteau. Laforgue himself
had said:

I shall take each painter who created a world, De
Vinci, Watteau, Michael Angelo, etc. . . . It will be a

series of studies in which, by an accumulation of chosen
words (meanings and sounds), of facts, of feelings in the
manner of a painter, I shall give the sensation of the
world created by this painter. My Watteau, for example, I have done by including a poem from
Verlaine's *Fêtes*.[31]

This is interesting because it anticipates the way in which
Laforgue is to write his poems, at first being a little irresponsible or at least light-hearted in his "accumulation" of words, and later finding a method that was more
discreet and disciplined. The article on Watteau has still
to be found. Six or seven other articles are mentioned in
the letters, the first being a review of Ephrussi's book on
Dürer for the *Gazette des beaux arts*, others report on
current exhibitions in Germany, and the most important
an essay on Impressionism, written to introduce an
exhibition of French Impressionists in Germany, and so
far unfound. Probably the letter to Max Klinger, written
in June 1883, though it conceals Laforgue's knowledge,
expresses his general attitude fairly well:

Not by reading books and "doing" the old Museums,
but by trying to see clearly in nature by watching, with
humanity, like a prehistoric man, the water of the
Rhine, the skies, fields, crowds, streets, etc. I have
worked more in the streets than in the libraries. If I
were not convinced that I have the eye of an artist and
am hostile to all artistic preconceptions, sincere and
desiring to instruct a delicate public, believe me I
would not write a single word.[32]

The interrelation of painting and poetry at this time
deserves a chapter to itself, especially, in Laforgue's case,
his indebtedness to English painting, to Ruskin and the
Pre-Raphaelites. Here one can only say that when
Laforgue writes of his first volume: "I insisted on the
empirical aesthetic of *Les Complaintes*,"[33] his move from

rhetoric to literary Impressionism has been by way of a first hand knowledge of contemporary painting.

On his own day-to-day existence in Germany, there is always the same kind of comment. "Spleen, spleen. How empty is life, here above all. I assure you I miss my life in Paris. However, it is more to my advantage to be well cared for, to have money, leisure, to travel, to enjoy good air."[34] The leisure which permits him to write also isolates him from the experience which might have given his writing substance: it makes him an observer of life, an outsider in almost the modern sense. He is at ease with members of the Court, but not strictly a part of it. Outside the Court he seems to have made only two close friends while in Germany, Bernstein, an accomplished "decadent," Professor of Law, a cousin of Ephrussi, and by many years his senior; and Ysaye, a Belgian violinist, whom he saw every day. But Ysaye had no knowledge of the "Complaintes," for example, until they were published in 1885. Attempts have been made by French critics to stress the importance of Laforgue's relationship with two women, Mme Mültzer, a blue-stocking friend of Henry whom he had met just twice before leaving Paris, and a lady at court, designated as R in his notes (but not, as Lindenlaub's vague recollection has it, the burgomaster's daughter at Cologne). Neither attempt seems justified. Though the searching out of significant liaisons could be called one of the constitutional diseases of the literary mind, critics have had to be more than usually literal-minded to make anything of his correspondence with Mme Mültzer. The tone of his few letters make this completely fanciful, as a reader may very well test by looking at the two most substantial letters to her (*O.C.*, I. 121–31).

His relationship with R, perhaps a lady-in-waiting, since he was able to travel with her freely, has been deduced, partly from the poems, but chiefly from cryptic jottings in a desk diary for 1883, published by

c

Jean-Aubry in Volume VI with the title of *Agenda*. These jottings are never more than two or three words: "Scene with R" or "Tenderness with R."[30] The *Agenda* as a whole adds little to one's knowledge of Laforgue other than the precise dates on which a dozen or so of his poems were written. All that can be said is that Laforgue's friendship with R continued at least through 1883, that perhaps he had her in mind when he later regrets not having married, and that a number of *Les Complaintes*, certainly "Complainte d'un certain dimanche," seem to refer to her. There is nothing at all, unfortunately, to give life and substance to these shadowy indications, except that it is hard to read the later poems without having in mind the possibility of some such crucial experience. After 1883, Laforgue's only reference to her is in a letter to Henry, in October 1885:

> I begin to think that it is my whole personality that has displeased the illustrious R. . . . One is not perfect. If I had known it, I would not have given you the useless chore of sending her my news.[36]

One would certainly like to find in the life of a man, who scarcely escapes from theory, something warm and substantial, a real instead of an affected, ironical relationship, but there is too little evidence for this to be more than suggested. Reboul's claim that the "Complaintes" can be read in terms of this "crisis" will seem far-fetched until there is more solid information than that provided by the Agenda.

His day-to-day existence, in other words, is interesting, but lacking many things that would normally be thought important: warmth, affection, responsibility, purpose. A reader of the poems may find it difficult enough to resist an easy equation between the quality of his life and the quality of his poems. It would be better, however, to postpone this kind of discussion until his progress has been traced in full. He creates a pose, and the pose covers the difficulties of his own predicament. Yet by writing he frees himself, to a certain extent, from his early, extreme position. This will be seen easily enough in the other chapters. For the moment, one could fairly characterise his years in Berlin by quoting one more of the many letters to Henry:

> Spleen, always. Your arguments mean nothing to me. I have tried so many things. Guitar. All literatures to this point seem nothing to me. A few pages of the *Imitation*, a few pages of the *Temptation of St. Anthony*, and in fact an anthology of renunciation. No, your arguments mean nothing to me.
>
> You tell me: love. I am unable. From my heart, I no longer can, and that alone would not be love. In my head, yes. But that would not be love either, and where is the woman who could inspire in me that cerebral love? With the senses? Less than the rest. With me, desires do not come with bodily substance; when I pass away the hours, I imagine to myself I have desires, but they are false desires.
>
> And I'm bored to tears.
>
> Luckily, I like poetry, books, real paintings, good water colours, scenes from nature, women's fashions, unusual characters . . . in short, the whole kaleidoscope of life.
>
> But one is limited and profoundly miserable when life has only the interest of a kaleidoscope, don't you think?
>
> And then: one knows nothing.[37]

It is Laforgue's accomplishment that from a starting point only a few degrees away from the morbid and the irrecoverably cynical, he first writes a volume of poems which catches at the interest of life's kaleidoscope with considerable verve and originality, and then moves on to write poems of the same verve which come close to an original seriousness, as well as being a technical accomplishment of some importance. There are first *Les Complaintes*, and then the *Derniers Vers*.

REFERENCES

1. *O.C.*, II. 89.
2. *O.C.*, IV. 119.
3. *O.C.*, IV. 122–3.
4. *O.C.*, V. 196.
5. *O.C.*, IV. 127.
6. *Stéphane Vassiliew*, p. 35.
7. *Op. cit.*, p. 78.
8. *M.P.*, p. 18.
9. E.C., II. 41.
10. *O.C.*, IV. 162.
11. *O.C.*, V. 146.
12. *M.P.*, p. 18.
13. *O.C.*, II. 58.
14. *O.C.*, I. 24.
15. *O.C.*, I. 23.
16. *O.C.*, I. 23. "Most people live and die without the least idea of the history of the world, its misery in the glory of eternity, its future agony with a moribund sun. The whirling of the universe, skies forever on holiday! Nothing, they will have known nothing. How many will go away without even having visited their own planet!"
17. *O.C.*, I. 34.
18. *O.C.*, I. 35–6. "Women howl through the night, writhing and biting their sheets, to hatch vile, unfortunate, ungrateful progeny. Half die within a year, not counting the still-births good only for concealing in the earth. Men, flowers, nests, all work without rest, for each hour of life is a bitter battle. And bad luck to the conquered, to the enfeebled, to the too gentle, to those too good to wish to howl with the wolves. Hunger, love, hope . . . illness. Then death. The comedy is always the same. And anyway three-quarters cry out: 'Not enough to eat!' and are for the other quarter a perpetual danger."
19. *O.C.*, I. 37.
20. *O.C.*, I. 37–8. "I spat on love and I killed the flesh. Mad with pride, I stiffened myself against life. And alone, on an earth enslaved by Instinct, I defied Instinct with a bitter laugh. Everywhere, in the drawing-rooms, the theatre, the church, in front of these cold men, the greatest and the most clever, and these women with gentle eyes, with jealous or haughty eyes, with which their exquisite souls might be chastely embellished, I thought to myself: everyone has

come to this! I listened to the disgusting groans of the coupling of brutes! So much filth for a three-minute orgasm! O men, be correct! O women, be coy!"

21. *O.C.*, I. 12. "No, I shall remain alone down here, devoted to the consumptive girl now dead, nursing my overly hypertrophic heart to the eternal fugues of Bach."

22. *O.C.*, I. 56. "Yes, this world is quite flat; as for the other, it's a fairy-tale. For myself, I'm resigned to my fate, and, without hope, to kill time while waiting for death, smoke luxury cigarettes in the very face of the gods. Struggle, you men still living, you poor potential skeletons! For myself, the blue meandering smoke which wreathes towards the sky plunges me into an infinite ecstasy and I sleep as though in the fading perfume of a thousand jars of scent. And I enter a paradise in bloom with bright dreams, where elephants in heat mingle in fantastic waltzs with choirs of mosquitoes. And then, when I wake up dreaming of my poems, I contemplate this dear thumb of mine roasted like a leg of goose and my heart fills with a gentle joy."

23. *O.C.*, I. 31.
24. *O.C.*, I. 15.
25. *O.C.*, IV. 53.
26. *O.C.*, IV. 91–92.
27. *L.A.*, p. 32.
28. *O.C.*, I. 55.
29. *O.C.*, I. 59.
30. *O.C.*, IV. 96.
31. *L.A.*, p. 22.
32. *O.C.*, V. 30.
33. *O.C.*, V. 131.
34. *O.C.*, IV. 154.
35. *O.C.*, VI. 228.
36. *O.C.*, V. 140.
37. *O.C.*, IV. 156.

CHAPTER II

LES COMPLAINTES DE LA VIE

The poems called *Les Complaintes* are the direct result of Laforgue's leisure in Germany. They are the poems of the conscious dilettante, existing in their own atmosphere of verbal virtuosity and imaginative energy. They represent his escape from the adolescent seriousness of *Le Sanglot de la terre*, and, in terms of development, his move from naked statement to an attempt at art. They are only a stage in this development, however, for when, later, Laforgue states that he is not a "maker" he means that his poems, whatever their verbal brilliance, are not arbitrary and artificial inventions, but authentic utterance, craftsmanship and imagination holding together. Laforgue learns to be a poet, nevertheless, by first being a dilettante, a poseur, a nihilist. He moves to the greater seriousness of the *Derniers Vers* through this slight, disengaged, and ironic aestheticism, writing poems which at one and the same time give his exuberance scope and yet let him learn to control it. This advance in his thinking about poetry no doubt derives simply from his being free and without care in Germany, and from his subsequent reading. But it derives more specifically from his interest in painting. His sustained study of Impressionism takes him by way of experiment to a new kind of poem, first to *Les Complaintes*, then to the *Derniers Vers*.

In November 1882, Laforgue tells Ephrussi that he feels himself capable of "A serious and compact volume on German contemporary art,"[1] with a long introduction concerned wholly with psychology and aesthetics. The essay which resulted from this thinking was published in

Germany but not in France. To Henry he wrote in February 1883:

> I am writing an article on Impressionism, an article which will be translated and which will appear in a German Review, at the same time as an exhibition by a friend in Berlin, who has a dozen Impressionists.[2]

Though this article has yet to be found, it seems reasonable to suppose that Laforgue's notes on Impressionism, as they have been edited in *Mélanges posthumes*, date from the same year, and that since, even in their fragmentary form, they represent a sustained argument, they lie behind his proposed essays, whether for the *Gazette des Beaux Arts* or for a journal in Germany. Nothing else in *Mélanges posthumes*, a random and irresponsible editing of Laforgue's papers, compares with these notes in importance.

In the section which the editor entitles "Critique d'Art" Laforgue argues the now familiar case for Impressionism; the avoidance of Schools, the dependance on the "natural" eye, the painter's closeness to his subject, and the importance of the light of circumstance as opposed to the artificiality of the studio. Most of what he says would constitute a perfectly good description of the poems he was writing at the same time: certainly it describes his intentions and his ideals:

> Where the academic painter sees only the exterior design enclosing the model, he [the Impressionist] sees its actual, living lines, without geometric form, but built up of a thousand irregular strokes which, from a distance, establish its life.
>
> The Impressionist sees and renders nature as it is, that is to say uniquely in a vibration of colour.[3]

With Pissarro and Monet as his particular examples, Laforgue links this theory with what (from Hartmann) he calls the "law" of the Unconscious, emphasising that the mind of the artist is not now an informing or a determining principle, but a means by which the truth of a moment is released:

> Each man is . . . a certain clavier on whom the exterior world plays in a certain fashion. My clavier is perpetually changing and there is no other identical to mine. All claviers are legitimate.[4]

This line of thought (the words of which remind one of the closeness of Wallace Stevens to Laforgue) is also familiar, as well as dated. The theory of Impressionism accords easily with his negative, atheistic attitude—his lack of belief—since all that one can know definitely is what one perceives at the moment, while the best that one can hope for is to perceive it accurately. It accords also with an evolutionary view of art, as of life, since in this flux of perceived truth, forever growing, changing, developing, one would not expect there to be anything fixed, static, constant or dependable. Everything is relative and art makes this acceptable. Furthermore, the theory permits a degree of consolation, since the observer has the satisfaction—if such it is—of being unique: there is no one like him for observing the truth of the moment, or, less flippantly, there is no truth without him, for what he knows is the only reality. Novelty is therefore important: the artist keeps pace with life, while, in the evolutionary scheme, the theoriser is always one step behind. The artist's originality in focussing all his skill to the task of holding to the canvas a single, ephemeral moment is not, from this point of view, merely a show of technical accomplishment, nor a withdrawal from seriousness, but rather an assertion of the artist's importance, since he is better equipped to know this kind of truth than anyone else. Laforgue argues for the new art as against Taine's idea of "santé," the remedial, therapeutic, and therefore rather unimportant effect of painting. It is of course not necessary to assess this line of thought, as though it were

the only possible attitude to art. It is enough to say that
the possibility of believing in the relative importance of
the artist's creative individuality gave him the release he
needed from other, more debilitating forms of determinism.

He goes on to illustrate what he considers to be a
painter's proper concern:

> To an ephemeral creature like myself, an ephemeral
> woman is more interesting than an absolute hero, in
> the same way as, for me, a man who wears clothes, a
> creature fashionably though ephemerally dressed is
> more interesting than the nude model for a sculpture.
> For myself—being human, incomplete, ephemeral—
> a tortured stoic like Leconte de Lisle, a nostalgic deca-
> dent struggling in a finite world, is more interesting—
> is more my brother—than Tiberge and all the Des-
> genais.[5]

And a little later:

> Dandyism, the beauty of a creature fashionably
> dressed, the propriety of the man, the art of the
> woman, and our faces which are so expressive, are not
> these just as interesting, just as solid, as human, as
> natural as a Greek nude?[6]

These, and similar remarks in the *Mélanges posthumes*, are
based upon Laforgue's actual acquaintance with Impressionist painting in Ephrussi's Paris studio, a knowledge which had been broadened slightly during his
early travels in Germany. When his theorising is over he
returns, as it were, to himself:

> The principle [of Aesthetics] can be reduced simply
> and solely to the need to escape from Boredom, by
> distraction, by novelty, by a series of minute and subtle
> strokes of a whip, by movement.
>   Render the living experience just as it is, and leave
> the rest: you will be sure of not making a mistake.[7]

In a way which is consistent with the new interests of
painters, Laforgue does not really have very much to
say about the function or rationale of painting, and when
he does move in that direction his statements are often
old-fashioned statements, made from a new point of view
and in a new language. Nor does this matter very much.
The attitude to painting as something to be done is more
important than the theory about it. Although all these
passages from *Mélanges posthumes* are close to particular
Impressionist paintings, and although Laforgue kept up
his active interest in art throughout his whole stay in
Germany, to the extent of being known by his German
friends, like Lindenlaub, as an art critic, and not as a
poet at all, a good part of his interest was to transfer
what he knew about painting to the craft of poetry: to
find his own way of doing with words what he saw
painters doing on the canvas. He wished for a poem which
would carry that same spontaneity of perception—without rhetoric, without preconceived form, without the
oratorical ring of the alexandrine. *Les Complaintes* were a
partial solution to the problem.

Almost as soon as he arrived in Germany, he wrote to
Kahn: "I have 1800 lines for my volume of poems
[*Sanglot de la terre*]. But it begins to disgust me already."[8]
Later, to Ephrussi: "I have realized that my book of
poems was a hotchpotch of banal scurrility and I'm
redoing them in a rage."[9] Eventually he abandoned
them altogether. "It seems to me stupid to try for a high
style and to play at being eloquent."[10] As far as is known
he made no attempt to publish these early poems. Indeed
he says, though perhaps with the affectation of someone un-
sure of himself: "To try for eloquence seems to me in such
bad taste, so low . . ."[11] and ". . . to publish poems is a
vestige of bourgeois habits."[12] In other words, the Grand
Style has gone stale. Just as Wagner was at that time
taking what seemed to be immense liberties with classical
musical expectation, and just as, simultaneously, Ibsen

moved away from what seemed formal and romantic, to a new, "natural" idea of theatre, so Laforgue liberates himself from what was conventionally considered to be a poem. More specifically he liberates himself from conventional French prosody, and, by doing so, leaves Baudelaire behind, (in this respect), and anticipates the surrealistic freedom of Apollinaire. When Laforgue says that he finds it stupid to play at being eloquent, he means the same as Wallace Stevens when he says, of the poet, "Be orator, and with an accurate tongue, but without eloquence," that is, do not abandon your sense of the importance of the poet, but abandon the rostrum of formal, and, by implication, pompous declamation. This entails, for a French poet, freedom from the rules of prosody, as asserted in various ways since Boileau, and for Laforgue it entailed a more complete freedom than had been achieved by Hugo or Baudelaire: freedom from the rules of syntax, of rhyme, of metre, and principally freedom from the rhetoric of the alexandrine. It may be thought, of course, that there is freedom within an established form, and that experiment entails, in the end, formal limitations more restrictive, to the extent at least that thinking about being free reduces the possibility of the poet's idiom being an integrated and spontaneous one. The case is not being argued here. Laforgue, like some painters, needed the freedom first, before knowing what to do with it, and therefore went to extremes. He used slang to avoid poetic or correct diction, he rhymed for the ear only and not for the eye, he departed from formal metre by imitating popular songs, and, as will be seen more fully later, did everything he could to avoid the distinctive sound of the alexandrine, with whatever romantic freedom it had been used. "My ideas about poetry are changing," he writes to Henry as early as December 1881. "After having loved eloquence, then Coppée, then Sully's *La Justice*, then Baudelaire: I am becoming (in the matter of form) 'kahnesque' and 'mallarméen'."[13] Besides this, he begins to write poems in which the words are not controlled by the sense, and are not therefore susceptible to logical or common sense rigour: poems, rather, in which the quality, tone, associativeness, and indeed the physical shape or eccentricity of a particular word is given scope over and above the formal meaning. In order to do this at first, he had to write poems in which the formal meaning was slight or in which ordinary meanings were flouted, and this is the very essence of his "decadence." In addition, it can be seen that this flouting of ordinary meanings is in keeping with his ironical and detached attitudes to life as a whole. The technical preoccupation is thus not a technical preoccupation only, as it was perhaps with Richepin, but a means of progressing towards an entirely new kind of poem. Looking at it from a slightly different point of view, it might be fair to compare Laforgue, at this stage in his career, with some English poets at the end of the century, who had to liberate themselves from the arbitrary combination of English speech and classical scansion that had been successfully achieved by some Victorians. The case is not the same, of course, since the English preoccupation with Latin metre was more obviously ridiculous. Nevertheless, the same instinct that took Hardy to metrical experiment and Hopkins to a freer prosody led Laforgue to his brand of determined iconoclasm. He had to be an experimenter first before he could be a poet.

Freedom-fighters and radicals have well known limitations, however, and the liberty which Laforgue takes for himself does not automatically result in good poems. At first, like Richepin in *Les Chansons des gueux*, he takes the rhythms of folk songs, street cries, barrel-organ tunes, and writes poem to them, which unite the ordinary and the serious, the ironic and the sentimental. The first step away from Romantic feeling was the exaggeration of that feeling to an evident sentimentality about which a play of irony was then possible. In the process, Laforgue achieves a greater "distance" between himself and his poem, the so-called artistic distance which will later allow him to write a good poem, and which for the moment lets him give rein to his inventiveness, without descending to the adolescent sentimentality of *Le Sanglot de la terre*. He calls the poems "Complaintes" and does not make extravagant claims for them. In many of them he merely plays with or parodies the familiar tune: "Le bon roi Dagobert," "Nous n'irons plus au bois," "Ma mie ô gué," "Le pont d'Avignon," "Tu t'en vas et tu nous laisses,"—and so on. "Complainte de Lord Pierrot," for example, begins:

> Au clair de la lune,
> Mon ami Pierrot,
> Filons, en costume,
> Présider là-haut!
> Ma cervelle est morte,
> Que le Christ l'emporte!
> Béons à la Lune,
> La bouche en zéro.[14]

It is not always that very much is made of this kind of exclamation, and the "Complainte de Lord Pierrot" continues in a more or less conventional way, interspersed with snatches of dialogue and song. The quality of the volume is to a certain extent given even by the titles: "Complainte de l'Orgue de Barbarie," "Complainte de la Vigie aux minuits polaires," "Complainte du foetus du Poète," "Complainte des nostalgies préhistoriques." There is even a "Complainte—Variations sur le mot falot, falotte." In the same way the neologisms are the most obvious sign of his attitude to language: Eternullité, sangsuelles, sexiproque, s'in-Pan-filtre, voluptés, crucifige, and so on. Similarly with rhyme. "Rhyme is above all, is exclusively for the ear,"[15] an attitude which results in matings like: le hasard/Histoire-

Corbillard; l'hameçon/poisson; dorme/l'Omniversel Ombelliforme; and fichent/affiche/Sandwiche. No doubt it was these outward signs that led one of the first reviewers of *Les Complaintes* to condemn the volume as "a veritable bramble-patch thick with thorn."[16]

The evolution of *Les Complaintes* was gradual. The book was published in Paris, by Vanier, at Laforgue's expense in 1885, and at least one or two of the poems had been written in the previous twelve months; others, again perhaps only one or two, had been written as early as 1881. Some are slight, insubstantial *jeux d'esprit*, or naïve attempts; others are more accomplished poems, contained within the idiom that they make for themselves. In November 1882, he announces to Henry that he has again begun to work.

> I'm working. I'm beginning to settle again to writing poems. I wish to publish (but to give only to my friends who are interested in my things and would be amused by them) a little volume of new poems which will be called *Complaintes de la Vie* or the *Book of Complaints*. They will be lamentable complaints rhymed like the devil.
>
> I already have five of them.[17]

He writes to his sister, Marie, in the following spring:

> I've abandoned my ideal of the rue Berthollet, my philosophic poems.
>
> It seems to me stupid to try for a high style and to play at being eloquent. Nowadays, I am more sceptical, I get carried away less easily, and from another point of view I possess my language in a more precise way, a more clown-like way. I am writing little fantasy poems, with the single intention: to be original whatever the cost.
>
> I already have twenty of these "complaintes."
>
> Life is gross, it is true—but, by God! when it comes

to poetry, let us be as distinguished as nosegays; let us
say everything, everything (it is, in fact, mainly the
scurrilities of life which must give our poems a kind of
humorous melancholy) but let us say things in a
refined way. Poetry must not be exact description
(like a page from a novel) but bathed in dreams.[18]

In July 1883, he tells Henry that he is ready to publish
his thirty or forty "Complaintes," and in August: "I
have now closed my 40 Complaintes (verse preface)."[19]
In the *Agenda* for 1883 he records the writing of eight
particular poems, between 22 Mar. and 30 Jul., and
from this, and from his correspondence with Henry, it
seems reasonable to suppose that most of the "Complaintes" were written in the early part of 1883. "When
shall I at last publish anything,"[20] he notes in the *Agenda*
at this juncture—rather a strained and plaintive note,
when one considers his previous insouciance. To Kahn
he writes in November: "I hope that my volume
Quelques complaintes de la vie will appear in February."[21]
Despite Henry's help, however, he does not find a publisher until the following year, and even then, because he
himself cannot raise the necessary three hundred francs,
and because of disagreement about the form of the
volume, the publication is delayed until July 1885.
During this period, between the autumn of 1883 and the
summer of 1885, it seems quite certain that Laforgue
added to his original collection: a few of the poems probably refer to events that occurred during this period,
and the final volume contains fifty rather than forty
poems. On the other hand, although he did add to the
book, Laforgue's development is arrested. The few
poems that he does write are more mature than the
early "Complaintes," but he writes little: rather, while
waiting, he contrives a dilettante existence, thinks about
a novel and a play, and cultivates his interest in the fine
arts, getting into debt as usual by buying sculpture from

Cros. His creative energy seems to have been stifled by his uncertainty over the publication of the "Complaintes," and Laforgue does not begin to write again until Trézenick publishes five of them in his magazine "Lutèce" early in 1885.

There is no doubt about the importance of *Les Complaintes* from the point of view of Laforgue's development: it is his apprenticeship. To attempt an assessment of the book in its own right is more difficult, however, since it lacks unity, and as has been said, includes poems not only of varying seriousness, but also of completely different dates and accomplishment. The "Complainte" is simply a loose construction, in which the so far unreconciled elements of Laforgue's imagination are permitted to exist side by side: his desire for originality at any price, his extravagance with words, his cultivation of symbol, his fatalism, and his Pierrot-like, wistful detachment of the dandy and aesthete. There is no strong poem in which these occur together, but one can do a degree of justice to the book by indicating selectively the kind of poem that it contains.

"Complainte des Pianos qu'on entend dans les quartiers aisés," written in May 1883, is characteristic. Laforgue brings into the poem the sound of the street, the cries, the songs of the children and the young girls, and the sound of the pianos, the sound of someone practising at a piano, in the same way as contemporary painters held on their canvases the changes of light and colour in similar street scenes. What they did with colour he tried to do with sound. The poem also characterises Laforgue's new attitude to symbol. The pianos, the young girls walking at evening, the suburban houses represent always his feeling for a life that is beyond or away from his, an exterior mystery, but then, much more strongly and definitely, his complete distaste for life as such, the mechanical procedures of living. "Listen to the bells after Vespers tolling out life in the provinces,

blocked up without hope of change, and the Sundays of
old spinsters,"[22] he writes in *Mélanges posthumes* and "At
my window, through the curtains, a piano regulated by a
metronome works away at the eternal Chopin waltz, as
stale as love."[23] The piano is thus the symbol of unre-
flecting gentility and of the automatic and mechanical
aspect of ordinary life, as though life were nothing other
than mechanical. In later poems, these symbols are integrated and made vital, so that in the *Derniers Vers* the
force that they have in Laforgue's imagination becomes
much more clear. For the moment, they are simply part
of the kaleidoscope: the activity of the street, the counterpoint of song, the refrain of the poet's slight, but wry,
fatalistic comments.

> Menez l'âme que les Lettres ont bien nourrie,
> Les pianos, les pianos, dans les quartiers aisés,
> Premiers soirs, sans pardessus, chaste flânerie,
> Aux complaintes des nerfs incompris ou brisés.

> Ces enfants, à quoi rêvent-elles,
> Dans les ennuis des ritournelles?
> Préaux des soirs,
> Christs des dortoirs!

> Tu t'en vas et tu nous laisses,
> Tu nous laiss's et tu t'en vas,
> Défaire et refaire ses tresses,
> Broder d'éternels canevas.[24]

This four part pattern, with its musical analogy, which to
the slightest extent anticipates Eliot, is repeated five
times to make the complete poem, with minor changes
in the refrain. It can easily be seen that if Laforgue is
indebted to Richepin for the example of *Les Chansons des
gueux* he attempts to do much more with the new
"genre," both in movement and change throughout the
poem, and in the extremities of contrast that he lets it

D

contain. Here slang is set against formal pronouncement, Laforgue's genuine concern against the lightest of irony, his feeling for the inescapable fatality of existence against his view of genteel girls walking back from church, at Coblentz, perhaps, or Tarbes. To Mültzer he had written in the previous year:

> I am living near the English chapel in the castle and spend my Sundays, like yesterday, working, with my curtains drawn, listening to the endless, lamentable litanies with their organ accompaniment. That lasts for two hours, during which time I'm wasted down with sadness, live over my life, my sad life, and dream of the cloisters. . . . Then the voices stop, I go to the window, and watch the whole English colony of Coblentz come out, among others a boarding school for young ladies in exquisite dresses, all pleated and starched, adorably thin and flat, and I find myself dreaming of flirting on fashionable beaches, by the echoing sea.[25]

It is the exterior view, the exterior attitude of the man set by himself, seeing everything not in terms of how he is committed to it, but in terms of how he reacts.

After its laconic beginning, the poem becomes more bitter:

> Fatales clés de l'être un beau jour apparues;
> Psitt! aux hérédités en ponctuels ferments,
> Dans le bal incessant de nos étranges rues;
> Ah! pensionnats, théâtres, journaux, romans!

> Allez, stériles ritournelles,
> Le vie est vraie et criminelle.

> —Rideaux tirés,
> Peut-on entrer ?[26]

Laforgue who sees life as an entanglement of necessities, or a succession, a "train-train," of fatalistic situations which leave the individual no importance whatsoever, imagines after all that the girl's song is satisfied and that the hero materialises:

> Il viendra! Vous serez les pauvres coeurs en faute,
> Fiancés au remords comme aux essais sans fond,
> Et les suffisants coeurs cossus, n'ayant d'autre hôte
> Qu'un train-train pavoisé d'estime et de chiffons.[27]

Laforgue never does enter this other world, and as for the girls, they are fated to a life of gentility, decked out in esteem, or embroidering braces for a rich uncle. Such is existence. Everything is susceptible to the drift of events and one's own particular complex of circumstance is the only reality. This acceptance, (which in a way stems from the same source as the more willing acceptance of D. H. Lawrence in rather similar, free-verse, evocative poems) is sealed, though lightly, by Laforgue's habitual and uncompromising pessimism:

> Aussi, bientôt, se joueront-elles
> De plus exactes ritournelles.
>
> —Seul oreiller!
> Mur familier!
>
> Tu t'en vas et tu nous laisses,
> Tu nous laiss's et tu t'en vas.
> Que ne suis-je morte à la messe!
> O mois, ô linges, ô repas![28]

There is no compromise in the "exactes ritournelles," the imposed patterns, which constitute the fate of these girls growing into the determinist situation, as Laforgue sees it, but this is no longer the didactic irony of *Le Sanglot de la terre*. Laforgue has learnt a degree of detachment, and although this poem, despite its liveliness, is still contained within the limits of a narrow attitude, it is a more fully accomplished piece of writing as such, more fully realised. He plays for the moment at being a maker of poems, and appears to accept the consequences. The dilettante is dominant.

A poem which demonstrates this even more strongly is "Complainte du pauvre Chevalier-Errant." Affecting to answer the question "Will anyone have the palaces of my soul?" the poet creates out of nothing the fantasy of an answer in the form of a wry monologue, beneath which, this time, the old seriousness is thoroughly concealed. Since the first volume of the *Mercure de France* is still out of print, the poem is given in its entirety.

Jupes des quinze ans, aurores de femmes,
Qui veut, enfin, des palais de mon âme?
Perrons d'oeillets blancs, escaliers de flamme,
    Labyrinthes alanguis,
      Edens qui
Sonneront sous vos pas reconnus, des airs reconquis.

Instincts-levants souriant par les fentes,
Méditations un doigt à la tempe,
Souvenirs clignotant comme des lampes,
    Et, battant les corridors,
      Vains essors,
Les Dilettantismes chargés de colliers de remords.

Oui, sans bruit, vous écarterez mes branches,
Et verrez comme, à votre mine franche,
Viendront à vous mes biches les plus blanches,
    Mes ibis sacrés, mes chats,
      Et, rachats!
Ma Vipère de Lettre aux bien effaçables crachats.

Puis, frêle mise au monde! ô Toute Fine,
O ma Tout-universelle orpheline,
Au fond de chapelles de mousseline
    Pâle, ou jonquille à poids noirs,
      Dans les soirs,
Feu d'artificeront envers vous mes sens encensoirs!

Nous organiserons de ces parties!
Mes caresses, naïvement serties,
Mourront, de ta gorge aux vierges hosties,
  Aux amandes de tes seins!
    O tocsins,
Des coeurs dans le roulis des empilements de coussins,

Tu t'abandonnes au Bon, moi j'abdique;
Nous nous comblons de nos deux Esthétiques;
Tu condimentes mes piments mystiques,
  J'assaisonne tes saisons;
    Nous blasons,
A force d'étapes sur nos collines, l'Horizon!

Puis j'ai des tas d'éternelles histoires,
O mers, ô volières de ma Mémoire!
Sans compter les passes évocatoires!
  Et quand tu t'endormiras,
    Dans les draps
D'un somme, je t'éventerai de lointains opéras.

Orage en deux coeurs, ou jets d'eau des siestes,
Tout sera Bien, contre ou selon ton geste,
Afin qu'à peine un prétexte te reste
  De froncer tes chers sourcils,
    Ce souci:
"Ah! suis-je née, infiniment, pour vivre par ici?"

—Mais j'ai beau parader, toutes s'en fichent!
Et je repars avec ma folle affiche,
Boniment incompris, piteux *sandwiche*:
  Au Bon Chevalier-Errant,
    Restaurant,
Hôtel meublé, Cabinets de lecture, prix courants.[29]

This poem indicates Laforgue's predicament in several ways. For a poet like Laforgue, irony and a full seriousness of effect (as opposed to actual seriousness) are incompatible. The thread of seriousness in some of the lines is not enough to justify a solemn reading. The abdication has been too complete. It may very well be that Laforgue's relationship with R is behind such lines: the *Agenda* contains similar remarks, similar in their impatience at least—"A great scene with R—she was born to be a mother"[30] or "In the afternoon after coffee, croquet with B or a scene with R."[31] But even if one's knowledge of the biography were complete, it would not affect the tone of the poem itself, which is too much of a *jeu d'esprit* for it to be treated also as a personal document. Attempts to make *Les Complaintes* a partial account of Laforgue's crisis with R, and thus suggest that the volume has what a critic calls an overall "architecture," seem too ingenious. On the other hand, there is a critical problem which is worth discussion, both for the kind of poem that Laforgue is writing here, and for the kind of poem that is written as a result, for example by Auden and Eliot. The irony of a poet always keeps one away from his precise concerns: at the same time it demonstrates, just as surely, that he is concerned. Not only this, it shows that he is concerned in a certain way. He is not involved in a conflict which is likely to be resolved, and the more sustained the irony the more certain this is. He is in a predicament, if one can ascribe any seriousness to it, in which what most concerns him is himself. This kind of irony is a direct descendant of the original Romantic ego: indeed it is, or ought to be, its last retainer. Thus, in this poem, the crucial line—"Ah! was I born, in infinity, merely to live here?" is balanced by the amiable foolery of the next and last stanza. Laforgue does not give up his old position in terms of himself, and the line, if taken by itself, still has the naïveté of similar selfconscious remarks in *Le Sanglot de la terre*. But in terms of the poem the line cannot be taken by itself. It is absorbed as it were by the poem so that the *cri de coeur* is a minor, not a dominant strain. It is, in other words, a *cri de coeur* which has been denied its force, like a romantic character in a play by Ibsen.

Irony and sentiment are made to complement each other. When a person adopts a tone of irony, of whatever degree, the irony refers back either to something which though discarded is still important enough to justify the new attitude to it, or else to something which though publicly rejected is nevertheless privately and nostalgically desired. In consequence, the test of the good modern poet, after Laforgue, has been to move beyond irony, since it is a negative and nostalgic habit of mind which prevents him from saying anything substantial. In Laforgue's case, the sentiment derives from the fact that the feelings he has are not in accord with the world in which he lives, and do not derive from it, but from his awareness of his own incompatibility. Whether or not this position is justified is not immediately the point. The point is that Laforgue writes the kind of poem that enables him to mature as a poet without the strain, as it were, of maturing as a person. As a result he is like Hardy, in whose early poems the most genuine feeling is to a certain extent devalued by being too closely associated with his fatalism. The man who trusts his own sensitivity, and comes nevertheless to an unfavourable opinion both of himself and of the world in which he has to live, tends (if he ignores or avoids the evident contradiction in his position) to lose his sense of proportion, and indeed is inclined to exaggerate things which to another kind of person are highly important but quite obvious. This is what Eliot did in his early poems. Nevertheless, for such a man, granted that irony is by definition peripheral, away from the centre of things, the habit of irony which is his defence against the world is also his defence against sentimentality, and the success of any poem written depends upon how well this balance is maintained. In Laforgue the balance is precarious in all but the best poems.

A second important consideration is Laforgue's attitude
to language. To oversimplify, he is the purist who takes
liberties for the extravagance of doing so, and much of
his usage is analogous to the recent preference for the colloquial as opposed to the correct, the slang expression as
opposed to what one was taught. In 1883, the degree of
correctness to be expected was great and Laforgue's
defection correspondingly violent. Despite the liberties
he takes, he knows perfectly well what he is doing: indeed
that is the point of it all—his attitude to words is what
Proust's was to character, where the eccentric or decadent is portrayed against the old "correct" yardstick.
The "yardstick" is perhaps for the most part implicit
and played down, but were it not implicit, the eccentricity would cease to be eccentricity and become merely a
strange kind of norm. When Laforgue first announced
the "Complaintes" to Henry, he said, "I already have
five: I will be very strict"[32] and, from the point of view of
a poet he is: that is, he does not lose contact with the
precise quality and effectiveness of the language. That is
what he meant when he told his sister that he "possessed"
his language. By the same token, when he is asked to give
an opinion of another poet's work, it is usually the loose-
ness of expression or the inaccurate use of language that
he exclaims against. He even tries to tease Mme Mültzer
out of the verbosity of one of her prose poems, by saying
that it is "too ornately phrased."[33] In his own practice,
there is a rhyming of language and imagination: the way
in which a poem is conceived gives a validity to the
language used, however extravagant, because a poem is
now a self-contained thing, and not just an attempt to
use other people's language better than they. Nevertheless, one of the differences between *Le Sanglot de la terre*
and *Les Complaintes* is that the latter are more verbal, in
the sense that Swinburne is verbal—not meaningless,
therefore, but relatively more artificial, and therefore
harder to penetrate. Laforgue recognises this very well;

indeed there is a playful poem on the subject, "Complainte des bons ménages" in which Art is opposed to his genius:

L'Art sans poitrine m'a trop longtemps bercé dupe.[34]

as opposed to—

Le Génie avec moi, serf, a fait des manières:
Toi, jupe, fais frou-frou, sans t'inquiéter pourquoi,
Sous l'oeillet bleu de ciel de l'unique théière,
        Sois toi-même, à part moi.[35]

The mannerisms of art are away from his true self, Laforgue is at the point where the distinction is a valid one, and the kind of poem in which "L'Art" and "Le Génie" will be inseparable is still to be written. It is not now Laforgue's habit to be heavy-handed, and the poem ends with the stanza:

Mais l'Art, c'est l'Inconnu! qu'on y dorme et s'y vautre,
On peut ne pas l'avoir constamment sur les bras!
Eh bien! ménage au vent! Soyons Lui, Elle, et l'Autre,
        Et puis, n'insistons pas.[36]

Because of the way in which Laforgue manages to give life to this natural, verbal wit of his, and yet control it, good poems like "Complainte du roi de Thulé" and "Complainte d'une convalescence en mai" achieve independence, as poems, rather than as over-intense expressions of Laforgue's sensibility. The first is purely imaginative and self-contained: that is why, of all these poems, it is the anthology piece. The second, "Complainte d'une convalescence en mai," approaches seriousness and gives hints of biographical undertones, but rises away from them with a self-deprecatory verbal frivolity. In the imagined convalescence, there is an imagined recovery and return to the banality of day-to-day existence:

Que la vie est égale: et le coeur endurci!

> Je me sens fou d'un tas de petites misères.
> Mais maintenant, je sais ce qu'il me reste à faire.[37]

Then the bitterness that was noted before:

> Elles vous sourient avec âme, et puis bonsoir,

> Ni vu ni connu. Et les voilà qui rebrodent
> Le canevas ingrat de leur âme à la mode.[38]

This bitterness, however, is not permitted to exist as such: it is overlaid with irony, overlaid in turn with a play of words, so that the seriousness, which is greater here than in other "Complaintes," is absorbed into the poem, and in the process is converted from a situation which one might care about to an attitude which, specifically, one could not care about. So one may contrast these two poems. In "Complainte du roi de Thulé" the metaphor is dominant: the poem gives a certain kind of pleasure, but does not refer to anything. In "Complainte d'un convalescence en mai," which has been chosen as an example for this reason, one can see the process by which the poet selects the art that goes with irony, preferring to protect his attitude with words rather than to change it. Thus in the lines—

> Je ne veux accuser personne, bien qu'on eût
> Pu, ce me semble, mon bon coeur étant connu. . . .[39]

(perhaps with a reference to R, since the poem was written in Coblentz) there is a naked, personal emotion which anticipates the consciousness of personal anguish central to much twentieth century literature. The irony of the title—it is in spring that he is convalescing, like an invalid denied what he was good enough to have—remains dominant, and the emotion is brought into control. It is brought into control by means of a critical distinction. On the one side, the loneliness of his personal, sensitive existence: on the other, the actual world:—"I know what remains to be done."[40] In this poem, therefore, we can see the poet putting life gently to one side, as unlivable, perhaps first from his personal point of view, then more generally. It is at this point that he is "decadent." It is at this point that he moves towards an aestheticism similar to that of the Pre-Raphaelites, or Swinburne. And it is at this point that one can see most clearly how modern poetry has developed. To write at all the poet limits his world and runs the risk of absorbing it into his personality, so that his poems are at first only that personality, and only with difficulty anything else. This is exactly the point, in other words, at which the poet rejects the world, and selects the imagination. But Laforgue would say nothing as clumsy or as blatant as this, as can be seen by the way in which "Complainte d'une convalescence en mai" is brought to a conclusion:

Je ne veux accuser personne, bien qu'on eût
Pu, ce me semble, mon bon coeur étant connu . . .

N'est-ce pas; nous savons ce qu'il nous reste à faire,
O Coeur d'or pétri d'aromates littéraires,

Et toi, cerveau confit dans l'alcool de l'Orgueil;
Et qu'il faut procéder d'abord par demi-deuils . . .

Primo: mes grandes angoisses métaphysiques
Sont passées à l'état de chagrins domestiques;

Deux ou trois spleens locaux.—Ah! pitié, voyager
Du moins, pendant un an ou deux à l'étranger . . .

Plonger mon front dans l'eau des mers, aux matinées
Torrides, m'en aller à petites journées,

Compter les clochers, puis m'asseoir, ayant très chaud,
Aveuglé des maisons peintes au lait de chaux . . .

> Dans les Indes du Rêve aux pacifiques Ganges,
> Que j'en ai des comptoirs, des hamacs de réchange!

> —Voici l'oeuf à la coque et la lampe du soir,
> Convalescence bien folle, comme on peut voir.[41]

The poet puts on his disguise in full view of everybody.

At this stage, Laforgue either writes a poem of extreme control, detachment and cynicism, like "Une Autre complainte de Lord Pierrot," or one like "Complainte du pauvre corps humain," success being achieved by limiting the nature of the poem, since the kind of detachment that Laforgue is capable of is that which goes with an extreme scepticism, as in the beginning of "Complainte du pauvre corps humain."[42] In these poems, the first effect is often of violent shock, sometimes of such an extreme kind that many readers can go no further. Thus, thought is "Elemental leprosy, senseless intoxication,/ Raft of Evil and of Exile/so be it." Nature is "an insipid sap factory with lymphatic scents." Spring is a "system" which comes "with its impudent crew of stimulants." These examples, however, are negligible as compared to the sustained cynicism of "Complainte des nostalgies préhistoriques"[43] in which ordinary people at their evening meal, "Ill replete with mechanical profits," have dreams of their private ideals, which are nothing but "Echoes of elemental First Nights," and which are consummated, as lust, "at the first fraternal croakings of the toads." Delivered from ecstasy, they clap their hands with a foolish joy, put on their dinner jackets, and go "to dine with elegance,/Then, among anaemic virgins/Assume a moronic air." This is the same as Ibsen's putting syphilis or incest on to the stage, and it shares the same advantages and disadvantages. The advantage is freedom from cant; the disadvantage is that of all explosives—they leave little to be enjoyed. Alternatively, if something more comprehensive is attempted, the surface or texture of the poem is often disturbed by personal feelings, which assert themselves just at the moment the poet is affecting to be free of them. There is the obvious bathos, for example, of the last line of the "Complainte des black-boulés,"[44] in which the "other person" has "Spat on Art! pure Art! to say nothing of the poet." Similarly there is the embarrassingly naïve conclusion to "Complainte des grands pins dans une villa abandonnée," a sustained piece of counterpoint in which the poet's memories are balanced against the mock oratory of a description of the storm, but which ends with the poet: "Alone, I shall travel fifth-class to Montmartre, far from my Mother and Father buried in Alsace." The mask does not fit. Yet again, there are some poems where this tendency is not so much a failure, as a necessity imposed upon the poet when he wishes to be his genuine self as opposed to a maker of poems. In the "Complainte d'un certain dimanche,"[45] which was written on 22 Jul. 1883 and which probably derives from his parting with R when she left the Court, his desire to be close to the subject for once seems to be stronger than his desire to cultivate a pose. This is the third stanza:

Elle est partie hier. Suis-je pas triste d'elle?
Mais c'est vrai! Voilà donc le fond de mon chagrin!
Oh! ma vie est aux plis de ta jupe fidèle!
    Son mouchoir me flottait sur le Rhin . . .
Seul.—Le Couchant retient un moment son Quadrige
En rayons où le ballet des moucherons danse,
Puis, vers les toits fumants de la soupe, il s'afflige . . .
Et c'est le Soir, l'insaisissable confidence . . .
Ah! jusqu'à ce que la nature soit bien bonne,
    Faudra-t-il vivre monotone?

It is clear from these various considerations that although the writing and publishing of *Les Complaintes* gave Laforgue the freedom that he needed, the poems did not give him any ultimate satisfaction. This is made particu-

larly clear in the debate he has over the "Préludes
Autobiographiques." Though they are in the style of
Le Sanglot de la terre, Laforgue refuses to give them up. In
July 1884, while he is waiting to receive the proofs, he
says, of *Les Complaintes* as a whole: ". . . I shall be able to
reread the thing and suppress the grossness that a vulgar
conception of what is strong in literature (eloquence!—
wring its neck, as Verlaine says) had induced me to leave
in it."[46] His reading of Verlaine's *Sagesse* in 1883 had
confirmed his distaste for rhetoric, but nothing would
make him suppress the "Préludes," despite his acknow-
ledgment that they are out of keeping with the rest of
the volume. It is as though he realises that the step he has
taken—in writing "experimentally"—is an unnatural
one, for him, and therefore does not wish to be wholly
concealed by his own art or artfulness (like the director
of a provincial theatre who cannot stop himself making
speeches at the beginning or end of a play).

In February 1885, he asks Kahn:

> Do you think, like the mathematician at the corner,
> that I ought to sacrifice this halleluia-preface which
> seems to me to serve quite well as a back-cloth, with
> its childish, outdated air.[47]

And in March, he answers this himself:

> . . . And I shall willingly keep the preface poem. It is
> made up of old lines, clamourous and pathetic ones
> —it is autobiographical. I sacrificed a large volume of
> my old philosophical poems because they were mani-
> festly bad, but nevertheless it was a stage I went
> through, and I do want to say, (to the few to whom I
> shall send the volume) that before being a dilettante
> and a pierrot, I sojourned in the Cosmic.[48]

In other words, the "Complaintes" misrepresent him: he
has yet to write his own poems.

This can be put in another way. While Laforgue is

writing to Henry and Vanier, it is hard to know how involved he is. When he urges the inclusion of the Preface, or attempts to be rid of Vanier's trade insignia, he seems concerned enough. At other times, he is more offhand, "For the destiny of an artist is to become enthusiastic about, and then disgusted by, successive ideals. My "complaintes" don't correspond closely enough to this ideal to satisfy me yet, and I am touching them up again, to make them less intense."[49] Part of this is affectation and selfconsciousness, no doubt, but at least from a general point of view Laforgue seems to have been aware of his own progress as a poet, and of the possibility of progress. Over and above all this, what remains certain is the importance of the actual publication. Léo Trézenick, editor of a little review called Lutèce, published three of the "Complaintes" in March 1885: "Complainte propitiatoire à l'inconscient," "Complainte de faust-fils," and "Complainte de cette bonne lune," and two more in June. Such is the nature of this release for Laforgue, as though, fantastically, his life as a poet had been given a stamp of approval (a reaction not too disreputable when one considers his isolated life), that within those two dates—between March and June—he had prepared an entirely new volume L'Imitation de Notre Dame la Lune, and within the next twelve months had written three other books, one of prose, two of verse. His apprenticeship is over. The indignant reviews of Les Complaintes ("Mr Laforgue is a Sphinx . . . for whose riddles no Oedipus has yet been born. . . .")[50] do not leave him unaffected, and indeed he replies to one of them in the well-known letter in which he distinguishes himself from Corbière (O.C., v. 136). But neither do they impede him. He is not so interested in Les Complaintes as to be unsettled by unfavourable opinions of them. He is more sure of himself than that. He does not immediately throw away his dilettante mask, but he does begin to cast around for another one.

REFERENCES

1. *O.C.*, IV. 204.
2. *O.C.*, V. 7.
3. *M.P.*, p. 136.
4. *M.P.*, p. 141.
5. *M.P.*, p. 152.
6. *M.P.*, p. 159.
7. *M.P.*, p. 176-7.
8. *L.A.*, p. 37.
9. *O.C.*, IV. 112.
10. *O.C.*, V. 20.
11. *O.C.*, IV. 164.
12. *O.C.*, IV. 186.
13. *O.C.*, IV. 66.
14. *O.C.*, I. 132. "By the light of the moon, my old friend Pierrot, let's in our costumes go preside up there! My mind is dead, Christ take it! Let's gape openmouthed at the moon."
15. *O.C.*, IV. 182.
16. *Revue moderniste*, 30 Sep. 1885.
17. *O.C.*, IV. 208.
18. *O.C.*, V. 20-1.
19. *O.C.*, V. 44.
20. *O.C.*, VI. 245.
21. *L.A.*, p. 45.
22. *M.P.*, p. 37.
23. *M.P.*, p. 30.
24. *O.C.*, I. 80. "Conduct that soul which has been well-nourished on Literature—the pianos, the pianos in well - to - do - neighbourhoods! The first nights, a chaste lounging about without an overcoat, in the complaint of nerves misunderstood or shattered.

    What can those children dream of, in the boredom of mechanical refrains? 'The schoolyard in the evenings, the dormitory Christs!'

    'You go away and leave us, leave us and go away, braiding and unbraiding our hair, doing eternal needlework.' "
25. *O.C.*, IV. 167-8.
26. *O.C.*, I. 81. "These fatal keys of Being which appeared one fine day, psst! to the heredity which punctually ferments in the unceasing turmoil of our strange streets. Ah, the boarding-schools, the theatres, the newspapers, the novels!

    You barren refrains, life is real and criminal.

    'The curtains are drawn, can we come in?' "
27. *O.C.*, I. 82. "He will come! You will be the poor souls at fault, betrothed to remorse and to futile occupations—the self-sufficient, prosperous souls empty of everything except a routine decked out in respectability and in trinkets."
28. *O.C.*, I. 83. "And therefore they will soon be playing more exact refrains.

    'Our only pillow! Familiar wall!'

    'You go away and leave us, leave us and go away. Why did I not die at Mass! O months, O linen, O meals!' "

29. *O.C.*, I. 118–120. "Complaint of the poor Knight-Errant.

Dawning womanhood, fifteen-year-old petticoats, which of you wants the palaces of my soul? Thresholds of white carnations, stairways of flame, languorous labyrinths, gardens of Paradise where your familiar footsteps will echo melodies recalled.

Rising-instincts peeping out at the chinks, meditations finger to brow, memories wavering like lamps, and Dilettanteisms —vain verve—roaming the corridors burdened with the pendant of remorse.

Yes, you will silently push aside my branches and behold how at the very sight of your candid air my whitest does will come to you, my sacred ibis, my cats, and oh redemption! my Literary Viper with its quite-effaceable venom.

And then, frail birth! O my Completely-Fine, Completely - Universal orphan, deep in your muslin chapel—pale muslin, or yellow dotted with black—in the evening my censer senses will blaze like fireworks at you!

We will organise such outings! My caresses in their naïve setting will fade from your throat with its virgin host to the almonds of your breast! O the beating of the heart's alarm in the lurching of piled-up cushions!

You abandon yourself to the Good; I abdicate. Our Aesthetics are complementary; you are condiment to my mystic pimentos, I season your seasons; we'll tire the horizon with stages on our hills!

And then I have tons of eternal stories, O seas, O the aviaries of my Memory! To say nothing of evocative passages! And as you fall asleep, in the sheets of your slumber, I'll launch out on distant operas.

A storm in two hearts or a siesta where the fountains play—everything will be Right, with or without your consent, so that you'll hardly have a pretext left to knit your pretty brows and worry: 'Ah! but was I born, in infinity, merely to live here?'

—But parade as I will, no one cares! And so I go away again with my foolish posters, a misunderstood quack, a wretched sandwich man: 'The Gentle Knight-Errant, Restaurant, Furnished lodgings, Reading-Rooms, Current Prices.' "

E

30. *O.C.*, VI. 235.

31. *O.C.*, VI. 247.

32. *O.C.*, IV. 208.

33. *O.C.*, IV. 131.

34. *O.C.*, I. 131. "Too long has this flat-chested Art deluded me."

35. *O.C.*, I. 131. "Genius has been coy with me, serf; swish on, you skirt, without asking why, beneath the sky-blue carnation of the unique tea-pot, just be yourself, quite distinct from me."

36. *O.C.*, I. 131. "But Art is the Unknown! Even if one sleeps and wallows in it one can't have it always on one's arms! Well then, this marriage to the winds! Let's be a Man, a Woman, and Another, and not insist beyond that."

37. *O.C.*, I. 192. "How uniform is life, how hardened the heart!

I feel myself crazed with a pack of small miseries; but I know now what remains to be done."

38. *O.C.*, I. 192. "They give you soulful smiles, and then goodnight! They've never seen, never known you. And there they are embellishing once again the sterile fabric of their fashionable souls."

39. *O.C.*, I. 192. "I've no wish to accuse anyone, although it does seem to me that, knowing my good heart, someone could have. . . ."

40. *O.C.*, I. 192.

41. *O.C.*, I. 192–3. "I've no wish to accuse anyone, although it does seem to me that, knowing my good heart, someone could have. . . . Isn't that so? But we know what remains to be done, O Heart of gold steeped in literary aromatics, o intellect pickled in the alcohol of Pride—it is by half-mournings that we must at first proceed. Primo: my great metaphysical anguish is reduced to the state of a mere domestic irritation: two or three local spleens.—Ah, mercy! At least I shall travel two or three years abroad. . . . On torrid mornings bathe my forehead in the waters of the seas, proceed by short stages, count the steeples and then sit down, being very warm and blinded by the white-washed houses. . . . How many counting-houses, how many spare hammocks have I in a Dream India with its pacific Ganges!—Here come the boiled egg and the night lamp: a most absurd convalescence, as you can see!"

42. *O.C.*, I. 146.

43. *O.C.*, I. 113.

44. *O.C.*, I. 126.

45. *O.C.*, I. 189. "She left yesterday. Do I not long for her? It's true! So that is the basis of my grief!

Oh! my life is in the folds of your faithful skirt! Her handkerchief floated down the Rhine. . . .

Alone. . . . The setting sun delays a moment his chariot in whose rays there dances a ballet of gnats, and then grieves over the ceilings smoking with the soup . . . and it is Even-ing, the impalpable confidence.

Ah! must our lives be single and monotonous until Nature is kind to us?"

46. *O.C.*, v. 92–3.
47. *L.A.*, p. 74.
48. *L.A.*, p. 79.
49. *O.C.*, v. 21.
50. "Lutèce," 4 Aug. 1885.

CHAPTER III

WORDS, WORDS, WORDS...

The fifteen months between March 1885, when Trézenick published the first of the "Complaintes," and July 1886, when Laforgue must have been writing the *Derniers Vers*, were decisive ones: he was no longer the hesitant apprentice. In the first period of enthusiasm, while away from Berlin in the late spring, he wrote a series of Pierrot poems, no doubt added to them a few that he had written earlier on the same theme, and sent them immediately to Vanier, his publisher, under the title of *L'Imitation de Notre Dame la Lune*. From this time onwards, he thought of himself as a poet first and foremost, and was able to dispense with a few of the poses that had come to be associated with his sinecure. Though nothing in his life was more certain than it had been before, he became more free of the feeling of uncertainty. In particular, he knew that he ought to return to Paris. During the winter of 1885–6 he busied himself with two further projects, a volume of short stories, later to be called the *Moralités légendaires*, and a new collection of poems with the tentative title of *Des fleurs de bonne volonté*. The short stories, though published separately in magazines, did not appear as a volume until a few months after his death. The poems, which were put to one side in the summer of 1886, when Laforgue began to write the *Derniers Vers*, will be discussed here with the poet's intention not to publish them in mind. A note from Dujardin, his next editor, seems to make Laforgue's rejection of *Des fleurs de bonne volonté* quite definite, though, before the final act of suppression, dismembered verses had been used to fabricate the little dialogue called *Le Concile féerique*.

In February 1885, Laforgue told Kahn: "You ask me for poems. But I haven't written a single couplet since the day I left my 'Complaintes' in the hands of the deceptive Vanier," adding later in the same letter, "But I have, I believe, splendid notes for my return to Paris: a volume on contemporary art and aesthetic theory in Germany."[1] The next few letters to Kahn are concerned mostly with the publication of the "Complaintes." Then in April he wrote: "I have become interested in poetry again." He had in mind, he said:

—a slender chap-book, something which would be a contribution to the cult of the moon, several little poems to the moon, a Decameron of pierrots, and on the associations of the moon during the day: pearls, consumptives, swans, snow, and baby linen.[2]

The volume published in 1886 is an uneven one. The title itself suggests that the poems were written over a longer period than Laforgue indicates in his letters: *L'Imitation de Notre Dame la Lune selon Jules Laforgue 1881-86*. Similarly it would be hard to understand why the "Lac de Constance" is mentioned on the title page if some of the poems were not written there, and it was in the summer of 1884 that doctors persuaded the Empress Augusta to break the Court ritual to the extent of spending a short time on the island of Mainau. It may be therefore that only the Pierrot poems themselves were written in the spring of 1885, though there is nothing firm to support this.

Although it is uneven, this volume occupies a necessary place in Laforgue's development. He had chosen against conventional methods and conventional styles in favour of the excesses of his own originality. He had preferred in other words the dangers of one kind of excess for the sake of avoiding the dangers of another. Secondly, he had been moving quite definitely towards the "pure"

poem which exists for itself and not only does without
outside reference, but makes it absolutely impossible.
The Pierrot poems are self-contained in this respect, not
statement, but nearer pure presentation, like a painting.
Thirdly, until this time, his virtuosity had been much
more highly developed than his ambition: he had been
able to do with words much more than he had needed
to do. By the same token, the "Complaintes" had con-
stituted an exploration of French prosody and an experiment in form. From now on, though he does not lose his
virtuosity and verve, his exact knowledge of the language
becomes more important than his dexterity in handling
it. Thus, the puns, neologisms, fantastic rhymes and
risquée innuendos, the outward signs of this old kind of
brilliance, gradually decrease in number. Part of this
change is recorded in the letters. When having to do what
all poets should refuse to do, correct other people's
poems, he cajoles Mme Mültzer into exchanging
pompous expressions for simple ones, yet at the same
time deletes the "neutral expressions" and replaces them
with "virtuosities of the pen."[3] On another occasion,
when praising a work of Klinger's he makes a similar
distinction: "It's done with great effort, very worked,
but so full of will, so profound."[4] And when he comes
across real extravagance he does not hesitate to say so:
"What do you think you're doing, reading *Romeo and
Juliet* in Riom! It's sheer insanity! locomotor ataxia! It's
inconceivably Bouvard and Pécuchet!"[5] These are early
and unimportant examples. More telling are his stric-
tures on Kahn's poems, which though put in a genial
way, as friend to friend, are not very inhibited. Kahn
should stick to convential rhyme and correct the liberties
he has taken with syntax. There is little point in taking
liberties if they look like mistakes.

The letters also indicate the general direction of his
thoughts. While writing the "Complaintes" he had said
(in the letter of May 1883 already referred to):

I regret one thing in the volume—certain necessary naturalistic lines, which I let pass. I have lost some of my enthusiasm, my naturalistic bent, as a poet only (the novel is another matter), (the environment in which I live has of course nothing to do with this reversal). Life is gross, it is true—but, by God! when it comes to poetry, let us be as distinguished as nose-gays, let us say everything, everything (it is, in fact, mainly the scurrilities of life which must give our poems a kind of humourous melancholy) but let us say things in a refined way. Poetry must not be exact description (like a page from a novel) but bathed in dreams.

(I remember, in this connection, a definition Bourget gave me: poetry must be to life what a medley of perfumes is to a flower garden) that is my ideal. For the moment at least. For the destiny of an artist is to become enthusiastic about, and then disgusted by, successive ideals. My complaintes don't correspond closely enough to this ideal to satisfy me yet, and I am touching them up again, to make them less intense.[6]

It is exactly in the sense of this passage that the Pierrot poems succeed the "Complaintes." They are one step more remote. The melancholy humorist knows the grossness of life and does not wish to exclude it from his writing: but the poems have absorbed this, and indeed all the knowledge of the poet, "in a refined way," and "bathed in dreams." There is no difficulty at this point in seeing how close Laforgue is in spirit to the English Pre-Raphaelites, since they also desired a poem which would satisfy their artistic susceptibilities, without sacrifice of what they knew. And it is easy to see in both cases that this desire is certain to be frustrated. If the intention to write elegant and refined poems exists as an independent, guiding principle before the writing of particular poems, it is more than likely that when they are written the poet will have to sacrifice "la chose telle qu'elle est." One cannot be an aesthete and live in the actual world, though one can be an aesthete and think one does. The man who writes such poems, the poems that aspire to the condition of music, or the pure poems of the French Symbolist, may well feel that he includes, with everything else, "the scurrilities of life," and indeed that the obliquity with which he does so is not only more subtle than what other people do, but also stronger and more definite. But this feeling relates not to the poem, but to the way in which he has come to write it. The aestheticism is a result. It is a result at least of his thinking about the world, or his experience of it, since there is obviously no such thing as a natural or spontaneous aesthetic attitude. Laforgue is perfectly well aware of this, so that though he nevertheless writes *L'Imitation de Notre Dame la Lune*, and for the time being chooses an "art" which is avowedly artificial, it does not seem that he was satisfied, firstly because he very soon starts to do something else, and secondly because he never relaxed to the extent of writing entirely "pure" poems, but has always refractory personal elements in them which refuse to be concealed.

The figure of Pierrot is a guise for Laforgue, not a disguise. He has always had in mind the Gilles of Watteau, the uncommitted, passive, perceptive harlequin: everybody is taking part in the masquerade that is life, and it is his destiny to play the clown. He is not Lord Hamlet, nor an attendant Lord; he is the Fool. To this early predilection were added literary figures: de Goncourt's *La Faustin* and the *Pierrot sceptique* of Huysmans. In addition the letters record several visits to actual circuses as his absorption in the symbol becomes more and more complete. This clown, who anticipates the unromantic, actual, suffering clowns of Picasso, is apart from the world, in a safe way. As a literary symbol, he is made to regard life with a detached, critical, but

unconcerned air, without priggishness since he is only a
clown, and without the romantic gesture of the desperate
nihilist, about which the Empress had teased Laforgue
when he spoke of Schopenhauer. The fatalism of
Laforgue's Pierrot is more aggressive than that of, for
example, Turgenev or Chekhov: it is more like that of
Strindberg, since he proposes, though with affected indifference, not the acceptance of life as it comes, nor a
resignation to the play of fate, as in Hardy, but a firm
negative. Whatever is contrary to life is his. This, too,
constitutes the rationale of the other dominant symbol of
the poems, the moon. Though beautiful perhaps, it is
not a romantic image. It is dead, cold, unchanging,
remote, not implicated in generation, unmoved by
gesture. Laforgue temporarily identifies himself with the
figure of Pierrot, and makes the ironical gesture of
adopting the cult of the moon as though it were as much
a religion as any other. Though this move on Laforgue's
part is a completely characteristic one, it would be wrong
to attach too much importance to it. It is an expedient
which lets him continue to write poems rather than
resolve issues. He adopts the "attitude" of Pierrot in the
same way as Houseman creates the Shropshire Lad: it is
a convenient and appropriate medium.

There are essentially two kinds of poem in *L'Imitation
de Notre Dame la Lune*. Firstly, there are two series of
Pierrot poems ("Pierrots I–V, and the "Locutions de
Pierrot") in which the harlequin lightly addresses himself to that other world, the earth, and ironically dis-
engages himself from the woman who wishes for a human,
ordinary love. The themes remain the same, so that the
poems are like the inconsequential line-drawings of a
painter, complete in themselves, but contributing to
nothing substantial. Some give him the opportunity of
displaying a neat virtuosity, as in the description of Pierrot in the very first of the poems. In others, the concerns
of previous poems are expressed without the old vehe-

mence and energy, but rather with a contraction and
economy of phrase which is almost impersonal. One of
the best of these is the fifth poem of the Pierrot sequence.

> Blancs enfants de choeur de la Lune,
> Et lunologues éminents,
> Leur Eglise ouvre à tout venant,
> Claire d'ailleurs comme pas une.
>
> Ils disent, d'un oeil faisandé,
> Les manches très sacerdotales,
> Que ce bas monde de scandale
> N'est qu'un des mille coups de dé
>
> Du jeu que l'Idée et l'Amour,
> Afin sans doute de connaître
> Ainsi leur propre raison d'être,
> Ont jugé bon de mettre au jour.
>
> Que nul d'ailleurs ne vaut le nôtre,
> Qu'il faut pas le traiter d'hôtel
> Garni vers un plus immortel,
> Car nous sommes faits l'un pour l'autre;
>
> Qu'enfin, et rien de moins subtil,
> Ces gratuites antinomies
> Au fond ne nous regardant mie,
> L'art de tout est l'*Ainsi soit-il*;
>
> Et que, chers frères, le beau rôle
> Est de vivre de but en blanc
> Et, dût-on se battre les flancs,
> De hausser à tout les épaules.[7]

The world is a scandalous place without a meaning, an
isolated event, like one of a thousand throws of the dice
in the game played by Love and Possibility. Despite the
laconic tone of this poem, and despite Laforgue's interest
in writing a controlled, dispassionate poem for the sake

of doing so, (perhaps with the example of Verlaine in mind), it can be seen that the cynicism is still shadowed by a lingering moral: it is "Ce bas monde de scandale." Laforgue is the man for whom the world is out of joint. He does not believe in the possibility of putting it right, yet he never comes near to achieving the amoral indifference of, for example, Oscar Wilde.

Secondly, there are poems in which the theme of the volume as stated in Laforgue's letter is a mere pretext for a flow of words, images and impressions. By association of idea, and by the reversal of normal expectation, Laforgue paints a word picture of an "unreal" subject, such as the topography of the moon, the effect of the poem being almost entirely in the words. This method has already been referred to in the previous chapter: it is here carried to the extreme, as an example will show. In the poem called "Climat, faune et flore de la lune," the poet, who describes himself as "vermine des nébuleuses d'occasion," says that from his Babylon he enjoys imagining what the moon is like. It is decadent in the most immediate sense, uninformed by thought, purpose, or imaginative insight, and one passage will probably be more than most readers can stand. Halfway through the poem the "inhabitants" of the moon are addressed:

Salut, lointains crapauds ridés, en sentinelles
Sur les pics, claquant des dents à ces tourterelles
Jeunes qu'intriguent vos airs! Salut, cétacés
Lumineux! et vous, beaux comme des cuirassés,
Cygnes d'antan, nobles témoins des cataclysmes;
Et vous, paons blancs cabrés en aurores de prismes;
Et vous, Foetus voûtés, glabres contemporains
Des Sphinx brouteurs d'ennuis aux moustaches d'airain
Qui, dans le clapotis des grottes basaltiques,
Ruminez l'Enfin! comme une immortelle chique!

Oui, rennes aux andouillers de cristal; ours blancs
Graves comme des Mages, vous déambulant,

Les bras en croix vers les miels du divin silence!
Porcs-epics fourbissant sans but vos blêmes lances;
Oui, papillons aux reins pavoisés de joyaux
Ouvrant vos ailes à deux battants d'in-folios;
Oui, gélatines d'hippopotames en pâles
Flottaisons de troupeaux éclaireurs d'encéphales;
Pythons en intestins de cerveaux morts d'abstrait,
Bancs d'éléphas moisis qu'un souffle effriterait![8]

Fortunately Laforgue does not do this very frequently.
Indeed only one other poem can rival "Climat, faune et
flore de la lune" for this kind of decadence. It is not hard
to imagine what is likely to happen when a *fin-de-siècle*
aesthete, never at a loss for a word or an image, lets his
cynical mind loose, by free association and without fear
of causing offence, on the theme "les linges, le cygne." In
the poem of that title the worst that one imagines
happens.

The volume has a final awkwardness. Just as he had
taken away from the integrity of the "Complaintes" by
insisting both on his "halleluia Preface" and on the
penultimate poem, "Complainte des complaintes,"
so now he spoils his own performance by revealing
his actual self, this time so nakedly that the reader
is almost bound to be embarrassed or offended. It is
as though Houseman had boasted that he had never
been to Shropshire, or Eliot protested that he was not
really nervous of meeting other people. In the last poem
in *L'Imitation de Notre Dame la Lune* which is called "Avis
je vous prie," Laforgue destroys the integrity of his
volume as surely as the schoolgirl actress who calls to her
mother in the front row that she has not really been
strangled. He fears life, he says, as he fears marriage, for
which he is anyway not old enough.

Oh! j'ai été frappé de CETTE VIE A MOI,
L'autre dimanche, m'en allant par une plaine!

Oh! laissez-moi seulement reprendre haleine,
Et vous aurez un livre enfin de bonne foi.

En attendant, ayez pitié de ma misère!
Que je vous sois à tous un être bienvenu!
Et que je sois absous pour mon âme sincère,
Comme le fut Phryné pour son sincère nu.[9]

Whatever Laforgue's intentions may have been, the poem is certainly not saved by the last line. Nor is the volume as a whole.

Laforgue's short stories, *Moralités légendaires*, are very similar in quality to these poems in *L'Imitation de Notre Dame la Lune*. Both the verbal texture and the imaginative attitude behind it are the same. Whatever their value, they constitute Laforgue's most important prose writing. Of work done before the winter of 1885–6, the novel, *Le Raté*, was unfinished and presumably destroyed, while *Stéphane Vassiliew* is an unobjectionable sketch of no particular interest in itself. After his return to Paris in 1887, he wrote sketches of Parisian life for Wyzewa which would be the disgrace of a serious writer if one did not know of his illness, and the book about Germany, *En Allemagne*, which is less dull, but from a literary point of view of no merit whatsoever. *Moralités légendaires* themselves derive directly, in spirit, from Huysmans' *En ménage*, a limit on their originality which Laforgue would not have tolerated in a volume of poems. When he first began to write these short stories is uncertain. He was probably working on them in the summer of 1885 and the following winter, for in June 1886 he reports to Kahn that he has enough to make up a volume. In fact he lists the following titles: "Salomé"; "Hamlet ou les suites de la piété filiale"; "Le Miracle des roses"; "Incomprise"; "L'Amour de la symétrie"; "Persée et Andromède ou le plus heureux des trois"; "Corinne au Cap Misène"; "Marlborough s'en va-t-en-guerre."[10]

The volume published, however, included only those "nouvelles" which had appeared in *La Vogue* or *La Revue indépendante* (with the addition of a story called "Les Deux Pigeons") and it is not known what happened to the other ones listed in the letter to Kahn.

The *Moralités légendaires* are anti-romantic myths. Thus Hamlet is more interested in the play that he has written than in what he calls his "domestic situation." In "Le Miracle des roses," Ruth believes she is miraculously cured of the curse which causes the suicide of every young man she sees—without ever knowing that yet another kills himself the very day of the "miracle." Salomé, likewise, having obtained the head of the prophet Iaokannan, tries to fling it into the sea—but falls over the cliff in doing so. In "Persée et Andromède," Andromède, imprisoned on her island, and in a state of high anguish, not because of her fate, but for her difficult puberty, teases the Dragon, the foul monster who loves her, disdaining the presents that he brings from the sea bed and engaging in all manner of theoretical *bavardage*. When Andromède throws herself on the sand, "clawing and furrowing it with her flanks, still legitimately deprived, then beginning to moan once again, both shrill and hoarse,"[11] the Monster tries to calm her by telling her the story of "Pyramus and Thisbe," but to no avail. She watches the triangles of migrating birds flying purposefully over the island, wishes to go where they are going, to love, but then disappears over the grey dunes, running wildly. "The Monster smiles in a debonair way and goes back to polishing his shingles . . . just as the sage Spinoza must have polished his glasses."[12] Andromède chases about the island until she is tired and wishes simply to be rocked in a cradle, until her head is filled with "maternal rhythms": but the only motherly lines she really knows are in a poem called "La Verité sur le cas de tout," which the Dragon taught her when she was young. It is Laforgue's evolutionary and fatalistic hymn to the Unconscious, and appears in this story as a parody of the Gospel according to St John. Persée comes at last. To give Andromède a chance of seeing and admiring him he engages in a little mating dance on his hypogriff. He is a superb hero and fiancé. He carries a mirror, wears sandals, has a rose lacquered on his chest, hearts pierced by arrows tattooed on his arms, and a lily painted on his calves, and he wears an emerald monocle, and innumerable rings and bracelets. This young hero is famously sure of what he is doing. Indeed his first words to Andromède are: "Come on, quick now, to Cythera!..." He decides to kill the Dragon by "medusizing" it, since he has the Gorgon's head tied round his neck, but the Gorgon recognises the Monster and with unbelievable determination closes her eyes. Persée therefore has to use his sword. Then the dandy, having done what was expected of him, admires himself in the mirror while Andromède laments the dragon's death. His first advances are repulsed; to Andromède's amazement he begins to yawn; he affects to think she is playing with him, and abruptly leaves: "Don't think you have such a wonderful complexion as all that!" The Monster, on the other hand, after Andromède's charming lament, comes to life again in the form of a highly eligible young man, the man or creature she had known before ("a good friend, accomplished gentleman, industrious scientist, inspired poet,") with, now, an acceptable appearance. And the moral of the story is: "Look twice, young ladies, before despising Monsters."

Though not alone in doing so, Laforgue anticipates the use to which myths have been put in the twentieth century. The old story or legend is not chosen for its intrinsic interest, but because it permits an ironical, mock-heroic play on the well-known theme and gives the author the opportunity of reversing the point or moral, in this case by proposing down-to-earth though fantastic alternatives for the ancient chivalric motives of the main characters. This is one of the ways by which a writer can ease himself out of the stock attitudes of one generation, or of a particular society, and, under cover of the fable and with the protection of the irony with which he handles it, explore alternative attitudes which occur at first as the attitudes of his characters, rather than as the moral basis of his own work. Thus one expects an interest in myths either at a time of change when orthodoxy is under attack, since the mock-heroic possibilities give an author the freedom he needs, or alternatively at a time when the author's relationship to society, not as a person but as an author *per se*, is a dubious one, in which case the obliquity of his handling of myth lets him avoid the banality that he sees elsewhere, his own actual stand-point remaining ambiguous. In Laforgue's case one could speculate that the novel that he would have liked to have written was a virtual impossibility, not only because he never achieved an unimpassioned, clear view of life, but also because he did not believe in the activities of ordinary people, nor in the motivation underlying those activities. In any case, he did not know enough. The stories told in the *Moralités légendaires* are loose fitting masks, exactly like the figure of Pierrot, so that they are much closer to being extended, dramatised prose poems than short stories. As expressions of his personality, they propose a view of life which is essentially passive, where everything is accepted as it is, where there is nothing better than what nature has to offer, and where the only preference would be for the gesture of refusing to take part, of opting out, of refusing to be animalistic, of refusing to dream.

Even in the last story, "Les deux pigeons," which is different in tone from the others since the two characters are led to realise and to acknowledge, though too late, that there has been something genuine in their relationship, there is a scoring of extreme pessimism and an exceptionally cynical and bitter twist to the conclusion.

The two lovers who had tried to avoid each other and negate their love, and who had tried above all to avoid the sordid conclusions of an affair, were brought, by the irony of life, to the same deserted spot, exhausted by their efforts to battle against instinct. A passing resin merchant, seeing them lying there half dead, was sufficiently intrigued by their cadaverous condition to take them back to town on the back of his waggon. They regained consciousness in a hotel bedroom, together. It was what they had intended to avoid. Though disfigured and made ugly by their experiences, they do their best to live as fate has ordained. Gaspard is particularly good, in his love for Juliette, at keeping up appearances. But she is not deceived, and realising what she has done to him, slowly commits suicide, as he does after her.

To a lesser extent *Moralités légendaires* anticipate the twentieth-century literary interest in myth as archetype. This is not the reason for Laforgue's adoption of a legend, but having adopted it, he so writes his new story, that the pattern or inter-relationship of character and situation tends to be Freudian, often by implication, occasionally (as in the character of Andromède with her love of the sea-Monster), by heavy emphasis. Laforgue's interest in psychology developed from his early reading of Hartmann and it is quite evident that he knows what he is doing. The epigraph to "Salomé," for example, is: "Birth is a departure: death a re-entering." From this point of view, both the themes and the details of the stories, have a double significance. Thus in "Pan et la Syrinx," after the momentary encounter before Syrinx is transformed, Pan consoles himself with a reed pipe, which is art; and, in "Lohengrin, fils de Parsifal," the hero escapes from his marriage bed, and from the incompatibility of the relationship, by clutching at his pillow which turns into a swan and carries him away. Similarly, Hamlet lives by himself in his tower and sticks pins into the statue of his lecherous mother; Salomé's

F

seductive dance ends with a decapitation; and Andromède stretches herself out against the cliff face in the
hope that a sea-bird will come to carry her away. But
sexual innuendo is to fiction as a dirty joke to a Sunday
outing; it may relieve the monotony, but it shows up the
exercise for the artificial thing that it is. The *avant-garde*
Freudianism of the *Moralités légendaires* does not make
them good short stories; nor does Laforgue's overall view
of human character, whether Freudian or not. The
psychology of the Unconscious as Laforgue had it from
Hartmann, and perhaps others, because of its assertion
that motivation is deep-seated and fundamental, may
help a writer to think about human beings, understand
them more fully, and become aware of the details of
behaviour which are the superficial evidence, if under-
stood, of real as opposed to superficial or formal character.
In as far as some nineteenth-century authors had been
concerned only with the exterior behaviour in a formal,
artificial society, the tendency at the turn of the century
to look for something more basic had, as is well known,
many brilliant results. In particular, this drift of events,
as Freudian psychology was organised and made explicit, led to a greater sympathy for the human being
as such, in his isolated, existential predicament, whatever
the condition of his life, and this sympathy, if not
sentimentalised, certainly permits a profound understanding of life, though it does not necessarily entail it.
But this is to anticipate too much. Laforgue has a notion
of the subject, but lacks the understanding that later goes
with it. His determination to remove his characters from
the world of normal expectation has the negative virtue
of saving them from lending-library silliness. In doing
so, however, in a *cul-de-sac* away from the moral and
spiritual actualities of everyday life, he creates for them
a world as unreal as the one they have left, and weakens
literature, if one takes it so seriously, by making people
into gaudy, papiermaché archetypes and life an activity

which, for a reason only known to decadents, atheists, existentialists, and saints, one cannot choose to live, but only to reject. Laforgue was certainly committed to the foolishness of this position, which is an illogical attempt to credit the individual with a degree of importance, and at the same time deny it absolutely. The stories, however, do not depend on these themes of repression and sexual frustration. It is Laforgue's ironic, humorous, anti-romantic handling that gives them their point, though the irony often has, as in the poems, a touch of bathos, and though the humour is more often sardonic than gay.

In any case, Laforgue's style gives the tales a quality which quite removes them from the world of serious meaning. Since the situations and scenes which he describes constitute only the fantasy world of myth, Laforgue is able to do with language what he does with the stories themselves. Normal usage is not important to him, except as something to be played upon. Extra-ordinary usage is the intention, and the greater part of the *Moralités légendaires* has the same verbal and imaginative texture as the ornate poem already quoted from *L'Imitation de Notre Dame la Lune*. Utter decadence is achieved, at the breaking point of meaning, as it were, when a word or phrase is taken to the extreme of extravagance, so that words are used as in the configurations of a masquerade, the spontaneity of language being altogether destroyed.

At the same time as Laforgue was writing these stories, or at least beginning to think of them as a volume, he was also planning a book of poems to be called *Des fleurs de bonne volonté*. As usual, the time away from Berlin, particularly the laborious weeks in Baden-Baden, gave him the opportunity to write. In May 1886, he tells Kahn that he has thirty-five poems for a new book; by June, this has increased to sixty. During the summer, however, his thinking changed, since by the time he returned to Berlin the idea of this particular volume had been abandoned. One of the reasons for the change was no doubt that he had found a medium for publishing what he wrote. The first number of *La Vogue* had appeared on 11 Apr.; Laforgue had received a copy from Kahn shortly afterwards; he had contributed four poems to the fourth issue, in May, and to the fifth, a prose poem, "L'Aquarium," which is in fact a few paragraphs from one of the nouvelles,—"Salomé." The magazine lasted for less than a year, but between May and December 1886 Laforgue contributed to twenty of its thirty issues. It has already been seen that the publication of a few of the "Complaintes" had a considerable effect upon Laforgue: the importance to him of this continuous publication in *La Vogue* could hardly be over-estimated. It covered the whole period between the spring of 1886 and the Christmas of the same year, a period of decisive importance in Laforgue's life as will be seen in the next chapter, the continuous activity of writing and publishing giving some point to his otherwise chaotic existence. The volume now known as *Des fleurs de bonne volonté* is not a book planned by the poet, however, and it is certainly not the proposed book about which he wrote to Kahn. It is an editorial publication, in opposition to the poet's wishes, and seems to be a collection of poems, as found in the poet's papers, presumably written after the publication of *Les Complaintes* and of very uneven quality. A good number of the poems are evidently unfinished. No doubt Dujardin, in publishing these poems in his limited edition, which was never marketed, was acting in good faith, since the edition was only intended for Laforgue's friends. One is anyway glad that it was he who did the editing, as he was more scrupulous than his successors. Nevertheless, in the available editions, *Des fleurs de bonne volonté* appears as a collection of poems of equal standing to the others, and this is completely misleading. It would be more accurate and more fair to regard it as a poet's notebook, in which there happen to be a number of good, unpublished poems. From this notebook, Laforgue drew off a group of poems to make the dialogue, *Le Concile féerique*, which he published in *La Vogue*. Other poems, as will be seen, are not poems in themselves, but the first drafts for the *Derniers Vers*. Others still are close parallels to the *Moralités légendaires*. The book, in any case, does not mark any substantial advance in accomplishment. The steps of Laforgue's development are so clearly marked out by the four volumes he himself considered as volumes (*Le Sanglot de la terre*, *Les Complaintes*, *L'Imitation de Notre Dame la Lune*, and *Derniers Vers*) that it seems unreasonable to flout his judgment by taking *Des fleurs de bonne volonté* too seriously.

The relationship of *Des fleurs de bonne volonté* to the *Derniers Vers* will be referred to in the next chapter. Apart from this, the chief interest of the book derives from the few good poems that it contains. Some, like "Album," which begins:

> On m'a dit la vie au Far-West et les Prairies
> Et mon sang a gémi 'Que voilà ma patrie!'[13]

are no more than versatile exercises. Others, like the first poem in the book, "Avertissement," are the competent, unexceptional poems of a writer who has learnt his own measure. In this group, however, "Romance" and "Notre petite compagne" are genuine, though slight, unimpassioned poems. So is "Ballade" which will serve as an example of the quality of the volume.

> Oyez, au physique comme au moral,
> Ne suis qu'une colonie de cellules
> De raccroc; et ce sieur que j'intitule
> Moi, n'est, dit-on, qu'on polypier fatal!
>
> De mon coeur un tel, à ma chair védique,
> Comme de mes orteils à mes cheveux,
> Va-et-vient de cellules sans aveu,
> Rien de bien solvable et rien d'authentique.

Quand j'organise une descente en Moi,
J'en conviens, je trouve là, attablée,
Une société un peu bien mêlée,
Et que je n'ai point vue à mes octrois.

Une chair bêtement staminifère,
Un coeur illusoirement pistillé,
Sauf certains jours, sans foi, ni loi, ni clé,
Où c'est précisément tout le contraire.

Allez, c'est bon. Mon fatal polypier
A distingué certaine polypière;
Son monde n'est pas trop mêlé, j'espère . . .
Deux yeux café, voilà tous ses papiers.[14]

To be discriminating in one's reading of this source book does the poet no ill-service. The poems are unequal, but the papers as a whole contain a wealth of imaginative thinking, or possibility, much of which is realised in the *Derniers Vers*. In particular, one can see that Laforgue's difficulty with symbol is at last resolving itself. The idea of symbol, as objective correlative, becomes important when the subject of the poem is the relationship between the poet on the one hand and the "external world" on the other, and the danger is that it will be either obscure, because relating to the poet's existence only, or for the same reason, limited in effect. An image in a poem which does not have this personal focus derives its force, not merely from the originality or inventiveness of the man who conceived it, but from the relationship, however remote, to some fixed point of reference, whether it is the explicit subject of the poem, the author's evident intention, or the reader's vague assumption of the stable world within which the image occurs. Laforgue is not a Symbolist in the strict sense of the word because the world which he imagines and recreates in his poems does not exist in symbol only, the imagination being paramount. On the other hand, the difficulty in all the early poems is that when Laforgue expresses a feeling as a definite image (like the pianos) too much is cut away for them to be fully intelligible or for the full force to be felt. He therefore has to discover a way of charting in definite term his wholly personal attitudes: he has to find a way of letting the image be the feeling, without concealing it. This he only really achieves in the *Derniers Vers*, where the poems are long enough for there to be an interrelation of images, and consequently a greater imaginative clarity. Because of its variety and freedom, however, *Des fleurs de bonne volonté* augurs well for the future.

A poem characteristic of the volume is the eighteenth, which is called "Dimanches." It is an effortless poem, its liberty less flamboyant, many of its lines, like the first, having a telling neatness. On the other hand, Laforgue at this time was in the habit of complaining to his friends that there was nothing to do but repeat oneself, so that many of the poems, like this one, lack tension, or lack the urgency that goes with a poem that has to be written. Partly because of this, the poem, though ironical, is not free of bathos, for despite a vein of parody, the last stanza is something of an anti-climax.

> Je m'ennuie, natal! je m'ennuie,
> Sans cause bien appréciable,
> Que bloqué par les boues, les dimanches, les pluies,
> En d'humides tabacs ne valant pas le diable.
>
> Hé là-bas, le prêtre sans messes!
> Ohé, mes petits sens hybrides! ...
> Et je bats mon rappel! et j'ulule en détresse,
> Devant ce Moi, tonneau d'Ixion des Danaïdes.
>
> Oh! m'en aller, me croyant libre,
> Désattelé des bibliothèques,
> Avec tous ces passants cuvant en équilibre
> Leurs cognacs d'Absolu, leurs pâtés d'Intrinsèque! ...

Messieurs, que roulerais tranquille,
Si j'avais au moins ma formule,
Ma formule en pilules dorées, par ces villes
Que vont pavant mes jobardises d'incrédule!...

(Comment lui dire: "Je vous aime"?
Je me connais si peu moi-même).
Ah! quel sort! Ah! pour sûr, la tâche qui m'incombe
M'aura sensiblement rapproché de la tombe.[15]

This poem was probably written in May or June 1886.
By the end of August he was no longer writing for the
sake of writing, but had in fact already published the
first of the *Derniers Vers*.

REFERENCES

1. *L.A.*, pp. 71–2.
2. *L.A.*, p. 100.
3. *O.C.*, IV. 102.
4. *O.C.*, IV. 135.
5. *O.C.*, IV. 190.
6. *O.C.*, V. 21.
7. *O.C.*, I. 227–8. "They are the moon's white choristers and eminent lunarians. Their Church is brighter than any other and open to all comers. They say, with their slightly jaundiced eye, their very sacerdotal sleeves, that this low scandalous world is merely one of a thousand throws of the dice in the game which Love and Possibility—to discover thereby their own *raison-d'être*—have thought fit to begin: that in any case no other world is worth ours, that we must not treat it as a furnished lodging in which to await a more everlasting one, for we are made for one another; and lastly—could anything be less subtle!— that since these gratuitous antinomies do not really concern us at all, the supreme Art is So Be It; and that, dear brothers, our best role is to live from day to day and, even if it means aimless exertion, shrug our shoulders to everything."
8. *O.C.*, I. 216–7. "Hail, distant shrivelled toads, on sentry-duty amongst the peaks, your teeth chattering at the young turtle-doves intrigued by your air! Hail luminous cetacea! And you, swans of yester-year, noble witnesses of

cataclysmic upheavals, as lovely as armour-plated knights! And you, white peacocks tensed into prismatic auroras, and you, stooped foetuses, you hairless contemporaries of those brassy-moustached Sphinxes whose pasture is boredom and who, in the plashing of Basaltic caves, ruminate the At Last! like an eternal tobacco quid.

Yes, you reindeer with crystal antlers, polar bears as solemn as Magi strolling along, arms crossed, towards the honey of the divine silence! Porcupines aimlessly burnishing your pale lances; butterflies with jewelled loins spreading the two folio pages of your wings; jellied hippopotamus acting as the pale floatings of herds in search of the encephalon; pythons like the intestines of minds killed by abstracts; shoals of rotting elephants which would crumble at the slightest breeze."

9. *O.C.*, I. 275. "Oh! I was struck by this Life of Mine the other Sunday, as I was strolling in the fields! Oh, let me but catch my breath again, and you will at last have a sincere book. Meanwhile, have pity on me for my misery! Let me be welcome to all of you!

And let me be forgiven for my sincere heart, as Phryne was for her sincere nude beauty."

10. *L.A.*, p. 188.
11. *M.L.*, p. 220.
12. *M.L.*, p. 222.
13. *O.C.*, II. 43.
14. *O.C.*, II. 57. "They told me of life in the Far West and the Prairies and my heart sighed: 'Ah, there is my fatherland!' "
15. *O.C.*, II. 41. "Hear ye, hear ye: I am nothing, physically or morally, but a colony of cells hanging together by sheer fluke; and this lord I call my Self is nothing, they say, but a fatal polyp. From my nondescript heart to my vedic flesh, from my toes to my hair, it's a perpetual motion of unacknowledged cells—nothing very solvent, and nothing authentic. When I organise a descent into Myself, I find there, I admit, a most mixed society which I've never seen in my domain. A stupidly staminiferous flesh, an illusively pistillate heart, except on certain days when, without faith, or law, or clue, it's the exact opposite. Come, that's enough. My fatal polyp has perceived a certain female polyp. Her world is not too mixed, I hope—two coffee-coloured eyes are her only passport."

CHAPTER IV

THE LAST POEMS

Even for a fatalist as determined as Laforgue, the last
year of his life must have been exceptionally unpleasant.
He made the decision to leave Berlin, lived in poverty
for six months, and died in Paris, in August 1887. There
is no doubt at all that he had come to feel more confident
as a poet, for *L'Imitation de Notre Dame la Lune* was published early in 1886, and during the spring he had begun
to think about his next volume, which if one relies on
Lettres à un ami was written between April and June. As
a poet, he at last discovered within himself the necessary
decision to break with the Court, with the boredom it
entailed, and the masks with which it was associated. As
a person, he remained indecisive. The distinction is an
unsubtle one, but there is a confusion about this last year
of Laforgue's life that seems to justify it. In the second
week in January, after his visit to Elsinore and as soon
as he had returned to Berlin, he began to take lessons in
English conversation with Leah Lee, an Englishwoman
who had been living in Germany for at least the previous
two years. There is a little uncertainty about when
Laforgue first met her since her address is entered, with
other addresses, on the back page of the *Agenda* for 1883:
but perhaps the *Agenda* was retained for just this purpose.
In the letter to his sister, in which he subsequently announces his engagement, Laforgue describes his early
meetings with Leah Lee, their visits to museums and
concerts, their discussions of literature and art, as well
as his own general embarrassment. But this is a sisterly

letter, as a glance will reveal, and the events themselves give a slightly different picture.

There is no evidence in the letters to support the suggestion that Laforgue was engaged in the spring of 1886. The extreme cynicism of some of the poems he wrote in Baden-Baden in April and May is hard to associate with a man who has just decided to get married. But he had decided to leave Germany, as he told Kahn even in April. In July 1886, he had reason to write to his brother, Emile, and in doing so mentions his plans as though they were already definite:

Now I shall be able to publish without fear.

. . . This time, once in Paris, I'll settle down there and never leave. I've already started sending my things. I shall stay at 4 rue Laugier. From there I shall publish as soon as possible a book called *Berlin in the Street* which I would never have been able to do had I accepted a pension. It is useless for me to stay here any longer. I have exploited everything that there was to exploit, and now I am wasting my time. I'm not saving money here: in fact I'm running up debts.

Anything rather than another winter in Berlin. I'm wasting my time without profit and through indifference I very nearly got married.[1]

Laforgue had already, in March, written the letter to Kahn in which he confesses his love, and which has given some readers a pretext for converting him from cynic to conventional romanticist.

At the time of my last letter . . . I was (but I am not really any more) absolutely in love with an astonishing and absurd little creature, an Englishwoman to whom you would immediately do homage.[2]

But even allowing for self-deprecation and pose, it is hard to be serious about a man who almost fails to avoid marriage "through indifference."[3] The *Derniers Vers*,

probably written later in the summer, show how un-
decided Laforgue was, in every respect.

As usual he returned to Berlin with the Court at the
end of August. It is reasonable to suppose that most of
the *Derniers Vers* had by then been written, since four had
already been published, and six more were published
before Christmas. On 1 Sep., he told Kahn:

> ... Were I to spend another winter in Berlin, I would
> come back indubitably married to one with whom
> marriage is completely out of the question, from my
> point of view, from hers, from everyone's.[4]

On 8 Sep., having already resigned from his position at
Court, he wrote to tell his sister of his engagement.
"Simply imagine the face of a child with a malicious
smile and large, tar-black eyes, always astonished, and a
little voice, and a funny little accent when she's speaking
French, with manners that are so distinguished and
delicate, a mixture of a natural shyness and a becoming
frankness."[5] This letter, which seems at first to be a very
full account of Laforgue's plans, is not to be relied upon.
He does not do what he tells his sister he intends, force
of circumstance no doubt determining otherwise.
Laforgue goes to Belgium, to the wedding of his friend
Ysaye, while Leah Lee stays in Germany to tidy up her
affairs. After this his life becomes harder to follow. To
Kahn, on 21 Sep., he says:

> I'm attending the marriage of the violinist on the 28th,
> and on the 30 Sept. shall return to Paris, very pro-
> bably with the pianist [Ysaye's brother].[6]

On 30 Sep., on his way to meet Leah Lee, he writes to
Théophile Ysaye, from Verviers:

> Ah! more than ever am I the slave of fortune. What
> can be called our normal condition is the grace of a
> total Intoxication which frees itself from restrictions.

...And I began to dream. The Corinnes, the Ophelias, etc., in our life, all that is a lie. When all's said and done, there are only little Adriennes, with long lashes, and a juvenile, ephemeral smile, little Adriennes with bewitching skin, whom chance (and is not everything chance?) has placed in our paths. Yes, everything is chance, for if there had been no Adrienne, there would have been a Leah; if there had been no Leah, there would have been a Nini, and so on.[7]

This lack of joy hardly augurs well for the future. Nor does his remark to Henry, four days later. "Since 10 Sept. there has been an enormous and fatal influence in my life."[8] In any case he has difficulties of another kind, for which the grace of total intoxication is no remedy at all. He is becoming seriously ill, and to leave Belgium, he has to borrow money from Kahn.

He met Leah Lee, probably in Brussels, travelled with her to Calais, and stayed the same night, that of 3 Oct., in Kahn's house in Paris. Little is known about the next two months, for he no longer had any need to write to his friends. He travelled to England on 30 Dec., was married to Leah Lee the following day, stayed in London for three days, and then returned with her to Paris. "I still had my three-month-old cold,"[9] he tells his sister. He has no money and no income, so that although "luckily the little creature I married has the good health of thin people, and is always lively and cheerful..."[10] they are soon in difficulties. The only good thing that it is possible to say about the subsequent six months is that Laforgue's friends, or at least many of them, do everything possible to reduce his misery. Dujardin, whom Laforgue had met in Germany the previous winter, arranges for the publication of parts of En Allemagne and gives him money in advance. Although Laforgue becomes too ill to work, Wyzewa creates the occasion for him to contribute, to *La Revue indépendante*, various pieces now to be found under the title of "Chroniques parisiennes" in the Connaissance edition. They are too slight to warrant serious discussion. It was also Wyzewa who contrived that Laforgue should receive a number of "anonymous" donations, apparently from various parts of Europe. Ephrussi likewise gave Laforgue considerable financial help. There are few consolations, however, for a man whose friends are obliged to become money-lenders. Laforgue, by June, is "all wrapped up in my room, happy when the opium in my pills does not deaden me so much as to prevent me from working,"[11] and his last summer, in the hands of a doctor provided by Bourget and a money-lender provided by Fénéon, must have been exceedingly unpleasant. There is no word in all that of Laforgue's wife, who died twelve months later, also of tuberculosis. Laforgue himself died on 20 Aug. 1887.

It might be thought that Laforgue was singularly ill-equipped for the venture he proposed for himself. He was a dilettante out of his element, still insecure, inexperienced in the normal concerns of day-to-day existence, and with a habitual fatalism which prevented his believing in the possibility of purposeful or decisive action. Most people are inexperienced in just this respect, but learn gradually under cover of convention. Laforgue's illness denied him the chance of doing this. Nevertheless, in terms of his life, one would like to have more information about the year before his marriage, since some kind of vital change seems to have occurred within that period. In terms of his poetry, one is content with the evidence that one has, since the tone of his letters so exactly complements, without of course explaining, the tone of his poems.

These poems, *Derniers Vers*, are the only sustained expression of Laforgue's mind and imagination. They have a stamp of authority which is altogether lacking in his earlier, experimental writing: in them he discovers his own idiom to the extent that it becomes purely speculative to imagine him then moving on to something else. It is hard to say at precisely what point Laforgue abandons *Des fleurs de bonne volonté* and begins to write a new kind of poem. On the other hand, having written them, it is clear that Laforgue intended them to be published together, despite the fact that they had first appeared piecemeal in various magazines. The text of the *Deniers Vers* has in fact an authenticity denied to most of his other publications, for Dujardin records, in his preface to his 1894 edition of Laforgue's work:

> A short time before his death, Laforgue, who had just entrusted me with the task of publishing his volume of prose, *Moralités légendaires*, . . . asked me by the same token to publish his most recent poems. After his death, therefore, M. Téodor de Wyzewa and Gustave Kahn returned to me the manuscripts that Laforgue had given them.[12]

(These are the manuscripts that are now in the Librairie Jacques Doucet at the Sorbonne.) It is in this same preface that Dujardin states categorically that Laforgue himself had decided not to publish or try to publish *Des fleurs de bonne volonté*.

There were several reasons for this change of intention on Laforgue's part. During the summer months he found a way of writing the poem that he had always wished to write, the naturally Impressionist poem, the verbal stream of consciousness in which, without artifice, the various facets of his imagination were at last integrated. Firstly, there were the *Moralités légendaires*. The writing of them let him feel his control of the language, and perhaps let him return to the writing of verse with his tendency to "verbalise" now under firmer discipline. Secondly, he probably learnt something from the example of Walt Whitman, for during the summer he translated nine or ten poems from *Leaves of Grass*. One can imagine that, as

he was interested in the kind of discipline possible in the
free-verse line, Whitman's version, where the power
comes from the mind of the poet and not from formal
accomplishment, would be quite congenial to him.
Thirdly, he had gained confidence by reading Verlaine
and Rimbaud. In Verlaine he found that one could be
free from the old rhetoric without having to be a perpetual acrobat or poseur. In Rimbaud he saw the force
of a strong imagination which absorbed all separate considerations into the integrity of a single poem. In June
he exclaimed to Kahn: "That Rimbaud was indeed a
character. He is one of those rare people who astound
me. How complete he is! Unique and very nearly without rhetoric."[13] Fourthly, there was the physical incentive of a new magazine to which he could contribute.
Kahn had founded *La Vogue* in the spring of 1886,
directed and contributed to it himself, and managed to
create a first number which included work by Verlaine,
Mallarmé, Villiers de l'Isle-Adam, and Rimbaud, as well
as the "Hydropathes" themselves, Henry, Bourget, and
Kahn. Laforgue contributed to the fourth issue, and to
two out of three of the subsequent issues, the first of the
Derniers Vers, "L'Hiver qui vient," appearing on 16 Aug.
Before this, however, that is before rejoining the Court
at Baden-Baden in the spring, Laforgue had made a
brief visit to Paris, and it was no doubt at this time that
he learnt about the magazine, and perhaps also saw the
manuscript of Rimbaud's *Les Illuminations*. It was then
also that Laforgue began to think seriously about free-
verse. Kahn and Laforgue, with the example of Rimbaud,
wished to write a poem that would be free from formal
limitations: a poem, that is, that on the analogy of
painting and music would have the form appropriate
to its subject, in such a way that it would be sophistical
to distinguish between the two. The poem would be the
thing itself: "la nature telle qu'elle est." It is not important to know who wrote free-verse first. But if it was

Kahn, he certainly did not do so successfully, as a glance through the three volumes of *La Vogue* will make obvious.

The twelve parts of the *Derniers Vers* are tone poems on the several themes of *fin-de-siècle* scepticism. They express the feelings associated with uncertainty, disbelief and anguish, not now in a dogmatic way, but evocatively, as though the intention were no longer to propose ideas, but rather to permit the world of Laforgue's imagination its proper existence, without the more juvenile emphasis and intention to shock of the earlier poems. At the same time, they are not listless, but nervously energetic, like the last paintings of Van Gogh. Their unity, for it is not a mere formality that they comprise one volume, is a homogeneousness of style, as will be seen. But it derives also from the two principal themes, as they are brought together: on the one hand, the various elements of Laforgue's personality, now brought to focus, and therefore under a degree of control; on the other, the painting of autumn, its moods, associations, implications. On the one side, the man now accustomed to uncertainty, sophisticated in that kind of anguish, yet still preferring the obviousness of being concerned, to the artifice of escape, whether to some form of eccentricity, like Wilde, or to a form of conventional living, like Hardy. On the other, the relative sureness of the poet, not needing to find a means, but having a means, having made for himself an idiom which will express fully, for better or worse, his particular way of seeing and feeling. The things which Laforgue knows are not now opposed in novel combinations designed chiefly to shock, as they were in the *Complaintes*. Nor is the irony merely militant. The poems are no longer floats with which the dilettante might make a parade of himself. On the contrary, they are the necessary vehicle of his whole view of life at that point, expressing both its substance and its limitations. Thus these poems speak for themselves in a way which the earlier ones did not.

G

One can think of the *Derniers Vers* as a whole by considering the way in which the author's own thoughts and preoccupations are gradually introduced into the complex of visual impression and mood. Whereas, before, the poet's thought had often been the dominant feature of a poem, like a demonstrator collecting round himself the paraphernalia appropriate to his experiment, now a whole way of seeing becomes the poem, of which the poet's own thoughts are at first only a part. The first poem, "L'Hiver qui vient," is almost entirely evocative. So is the second, "Le Mystère des trois cors." Nature is conceived of as a compelling, but automatic system, (random fertilisation, a meaningless life, death) and the cause of all this, the sun, is now itself dead, as though hunted to death across the autumn landscape, its previous splendour nothing but a mockery. After the sound of the hunting horns, there is winter, the poet's season. In the third poem, "Dimanches," the personal element becomes more strong. The poet, though he wishes to believe in love, sees himself as a "pale, poor, paltry individual,"[14] who cannot even believe in himself. Perhaps he wishes to believe in a real engagement, a real marriage, (for if one read this out of context it might very well appear autobiographical), but what he actually sees are the symbols of an alien world, Sundays, pianos, genteel dresses, and the young girl returning home after church, who "knows her past to be quite different to his."[15] He also fears lust, for marriage would lead only to the "adoration of incurable organs."[16] Because of the hopelessness of this, the girl should not accommodate herself to life; there should be the same rupture as between Hamlet and Ophelia; and the poet should go for a little walk to get rid of his spleen. In the next poem, also called "Dimanches," the balance is redressed. He plays ironically with a view of the same symbol, the convent girl "always ready for the Mass they make a game of,"[17] but this time more remotely, for he himself is a Polar Bear:

Je suis venu par ces banquises
Plus pures que les communiantes en blanc . . .
Moi, je ne vais pas à l'église,
Moi, je suis le Grand Chancelier de l'Analyse,
Qu'on se le dise.[18]

The fifth poem, "Pétition," sustains the same balance. The absolute pure love for which the poet has been craving is unobtainable. It is an empty square, without a fountain in it, from which, at the ends of the streets which lead away in different directions, the life that other people lead is seen and heard distantly. "Mais, à tous les bouts, d'étourdissantes fêtes foraines."[19] There are no absolutes, only compromise. "Tout est pas plus, tout est permis."[20] That is to say, in the old determinist *impasse*, only what is permitted is permitted, and the individual can conceive of no life for himself outside the rigid scheme of things he sees more and more clearly the more he thinks. Despite this knowledge, however, there is still a desire for a genuine existence, and this is the subject of the sixth poem, "Simple Agonie." The sensibility which makes the poet a pariah and sets him away from the world also inclines him to "les sympathies de mai,"[21] so that his poems are ambiguous, insubstantial things, like the life of an insect. Laforgue in these poems, in other words, is that very modern figure who lets the weaknesses of his own personality be the lens through which a faithful credible view is achieved. In moral art the limitations of personality weaken the impact of the work; in art which is taking care not to be moral, but has a different ambition, in this case impressionistic, a character who is sensitive even in an anaemic way is taken to be a greater guarantee of authenticity than his more heroic predecessors.

The next poem, "Solo de lune," is the recapitulation, as in music. After loving like fools, they had parted without saying a word, both wishing, apparently, for a spontaneous, causeless, un-sordid love, or nothing at all, and the poet for his part so soured by the world as to be unable to act in it. "A feeling of spleen kept me remote/ and this feeling derived from everything."[22] This is seen, imagined, while the poet lies smoking on top of a coach which is travelling through the night, so that he is again the isolated observer remote in the darkness from the roads, the lighted houses, the hotels, the coach stops which they pass. There is again the feeling of his being apart from the rest—"What profound and decent bed-rooms!"[23] And there is the same plaintive loneliness: "No-one awaits me, I am visiting no-one./I have nothing but the friendships of hotel bedrooms,"[24] the sentiment being balanced by the final irony:

> J'eusse été le modèle des époux!
> Comme le frou-frou de ta robe est le modèle des frou-frou.[25]

The relationship between the two poeple who might have been lovers is then expressed within the dramatic context of discussion or argument, in very much the same way as Eliot in *The Waste Land*. In "Légende" it is the woman who argues with the man to make him or let him feel that there is something more than exile, at least "the sweetness of legend." The ninth and tenth poems were published together in *La Vogue* as "Les Amours." First there is another dramatic situation, again from the point of view of the woman, who, as sure of love as "Du vide insensé de mon coeur," could come "to curl herself up on the mattress I have put for this purpose outside my door,"[26] whereas the poet, in the next poem, laments the fact that his life has been spent on the quayside, always just failing to embark on "quite tragic episodes/and all of it for Love."[27] The attitude of Laforgue here, or his poetic *döppelganger*, is summarised more firmly by Eliot in "The Love Song of J. Alfred Prufrock": "Do I dare? —Do I dare disturb the Universe?" while Hamlet's appearance in that poem, (though rather arbitrarily referring back to the source, in Laforgue) shows the difference between the two men. Laforgue, with a Hamlet who is driven to disgust by the sordidness of the world, does not quite learn to disengage himself from the actual situation, and so remains too involved in sentiment though it is expressed now in dramatic form. Eliot, on the other hand, distinguishes himself from Hamlet and that kind of concern, so letting the drama of the poem have greater impact. Though Eliot proves much more adroit at the technique which Laforgue is discovering, the reason they are both interested in that technique is that they are both in the same situation: they wish to write a personal poem in a safe impersonal way. There is no such thing as an impersonal fatalism, however, and though the detachment of the *Derniers Vers* is greater than in the other poems, it is not by any means complete. Love in consequence is reduced to the arbitrary coupling, according to circumstance, of "A, B, C, or D," the poet in the end feeling only his own loneliness:

> Et je ne serais qu'un pis-aller,
> Comme l'est mon jour dans le Temps,
> Comme l'est ma place dans l'Espace;
> Et l'on ne voudrait pas que je m'accommodasse
> De ce sort vraiment dégoûtant! . . .[28]

At this point one can see more clearly why the story of Hamlet was congenial to Laforgue. Hamlet, in this reading, gave up Ophelia because he did not wish to accommodate himself to an existence which was irretrievably sordid and futile, and urged Ophelia to a convent for the same reason, because of his love. So the twelfth of the *Derniers Vers* has as epigraph Hamlet's speech to Ophelia, beginning with the words: "Get thee to a nunnery: why wouldst thou be a breeder of sinners?" In this context the poet recalls his home town:

Un couvent dans ma ville natale
Douce de vingt mille âmes à peine,
Entre le lycée et la préfecture,
Et vis à vis la cathédrale . . .[29]

and, rather than consign his lover to such a fate, prefers
to be "two in the chimney corner," resigned to the
"fatalistic hymn" of existence and still seeing it as "a
deafening fairground"—"Frailty thy name is woman:
everything's routine."[30] The poem then ends with lines
which, despite the reference to Baudelaire, would be
hollow indeed without the substance of twelve poems
behind them:

O Nature, donne-moi la force et le courage
De me croire en age,
O Nature, relève-moi le front!
Puisque, tôt ou tard, nous mourrons. . . .[31]

To follow one of the principal themes through a
number of poems is only one of several possible lines of
approach. In Laforgue's case, nevertheless, it seems important to stress that he had at least achieved something
a good deal more substantial than the previous "kaleidoscope" poems. The unity is of course not only of theme.
It is much more an imaginative unity, since Laforgue's
experiences are to a greater extent translated into a visual
and a musical idiom, away from the naïveté of plain
statement, if not wholly free of personal bathos.

This becomes clear as soon as one looks closely at any
particular poem. Whatever reservations it might be
necessary to have about Laforgue himself, there is no
doubt that many of these poems are highly accomplished
works. The first poem, for example, "L'Hiver qui vient,"
is one of the most complex and powerful. A series of
exclamations, free from the restriction of grammar, like
the brusque, non-realistic strokes of the Impressionist
painter, sketch in the atmosphere, but with a play upon
words that perhaps takes the imagination by surprise. It

is not the Continental system and a naval blockade in the
real emergency of the Napoleonic War, but in the poet's
emergency a blockade of sentiment, in which the poet's
mind is trapped by the impressions of autumn, by
packets from the Levant. At the same time, there is the
habit of irony, and a literary self-consciousness: not the
rich mists of the Keatsian autumn, but the mist of the
factory chimneys in a drizzling rain.

> Blocus sentimental! Messageries du Levant! . . .
> Oh! tombée de la pluie! Oh! tombée de la nuit,
> Oh! le vent! . . .
> La Toussaint, la Noël, et la Nouvelle Année,
> Oh, dans les bruines, toutes mes cheminées! . . .
> D'usines. . . .[32]

Then with the easy assonance of the following lines, two
further themes or metaphors are introduced; the sound
of the hunting horn, the primitive image of life being
hunted to death, and the effect of water, the woods
literally brown and rusted away by rain, so that one can
no longer shelter beneath the trees in the park.

> On ne peut plus s'asseoir, tous les bancs sont mouillés;
> Crois-moi, c'est bien fini jusqu'à l'année prochaine,
> Tous les bancs sont mouillés, tant les bois sont rouillés,
> Et tant les cors ont fait ton ton, ont fait ton taine! . . .
>
> Ah! nuées accourues des côtes de la Manche,
> Vous nous avez gâté notre dernier dimanche.[33]

Already it is evident that the theoretical images of
Laforgue's earlier poems have been replaced by definite
and usually visual ones. This is an improvement in itself.
It means also, however, that his virtuosity with words
and his inventiveness have a much more substantial
imaginative base. Thus in the line which follows he can
allow himself to play with words in an attempt to conjure
up verbally the nostalgic calls of the hunt. The thread of

irony also continues: the great suns, the world's glorious progenitors, have been occupied with nothing greater than agricultural shows. But in spite of this play of words, the passage is held to its three dominant images. The listless atmosphere of the damp autumn day weights with heavy drops of water the spider-webs, the symbols of ephemeral existence. The sun, exhausted and spent and as white as spittle, lies on his coat in the yellow broom, unable to go further than the top of the hill, despite the approach of the hunt. Finally, lying there, it shudders like a gland torn from the neck—as though the hounds had finally got their prey—with nobody at hand to help.

> Il bruine;
> Dans la forêt mouillée, les toiles d'araignées
> Ploient sous les gouttes d'eau, et c'est leur ruine.
> Soleils plénipotentiaires des travaux en blonds Pactoles
> Des spectacles agricoles,
> Où êtes-vous ensevelis?
> Ce soir un soleil fichu gît au haut du coteau,
> Gît sur le flanc, dans les genêts, sur son manteau.
> Un soleil blanc somme un crachat d'estaminet
> Sur une litière de jaunes genêts d'automne.
> Et les cors lui sonnent!
> Qu'il revienne . . .
> Qu'il revienne à lui! . . .
> Taïaut! Taïaut! et hallali!
> O triste antienne, as-tu fini! . . .
> Et font les fous! . . .
> Et il gît là, comme une glande arrachée dans un cou.
> Et il frissonne, sans personne! . . .[34]

Only in the next section, after forty lines or so, and after the fine Blockade image of patrols of clouds being harried away, like sheep to the fold, or like emigrés across the Atlantic, so escaping the tyranny of winter, does the poet introduce a further more personal theme. Both the high winds that work havoc in the little gardens (which with the adjective "modestes" becomes the genteel, conventional gardens of "those other people"), and the noise of the axes echoing in the woods, are the poet's sounds. It is the destruction he knows.

Allons, allons, et hallali!

C'est l'Hiver bien connu qui s'amène;
Oh! les tournants des grandes routes,
Et sans petit Chaperon Rouge qui chemine!...
Oh! leurs ornières des chars de l'autre mois,
Montant en don quichottesques rails
Vers les patrouilles des nuées en déroute
Que le vent malmène vers les transatlantiques bercails!...
Accélérons, accélérons, c'est la saison bien connue, cette fois
Et le vent, cette nuit, il en a fait de belles!
O dégâts, ô nids, ô modestes jardinets!
Mon coeur et mon sommeil: ô échos des cognées!...[35]

These themes and impressions are followed by a succession of associations. The branches which have lost their green leaves cover an undergrowth which is a compost of dead leaves, leaves which go flying to the lakes, or to the bonfires, or, with a sudden awkwardness, a jarring extension of the Blockade image, to the mattresses for French soldiers overseas. Communications are cut. The rust eats at the telegraph wires. And over all, there is the sound of the hunt, but going away now, on the North Wind.

Tous ces rameaux avaient encor leurs feuilles vertes,
Les sous-bois ne sont plus qu'un fumier de feuilles mortes;
Feuilles, folioles, qu'un bon vent vous emporte
Vers les étangs par ribambelles,
Ou pour le feu du garde-chasse,

Ou les sommiers des ambulances
Pour les soldats loin de la France.

C'est la saison, c'est la saison, la rouille envahit les
    masses,
La rouille ronge en leurs spleens kilométriques
Les fils télégraphiques des grandes routes où nul ne
    passe.

Les cors, les cors, les cors—mélancoliques!...
Mélancoliques!...
S'en vont, changeant de ton,
Changeant de ton et de musique,

Ton, ton, ton taine, ton ton!...
Les cors, les cors, les cors!...
S'en sont allés au vent du Nord.

Je ne puis quitter ce ton: que d'échos!...[36]

Towards the end, the easy fluency and suggestiveness
of the tone poem is stiffened in several ways. Firstly, there
is a reference to a painting of Watteau, with a description
of elegant dancers beneath the chestnut trees in autumn,
which reminds one of Watteau's painting, "Le Repos de
chasse," in the Wallace collection. This is another of the
techniques later adopted by Eliot. Watteau made a
world, and that eighteenth century elegance is now
brought into the poem as a point of reference against
which is seen the poet's modern world: the loneliness and
suffering of people without hearth and home.

C'est la saison, c'est la saison, adieu vendanges!...
Voici venir les pluies d'une patience d'ange,
Adieu vendanges, et adieu tous les paniers,
Tous les paniers Watteau des bourrées sous les mar-
    ronniers,
C'est la toux dans les dortoirs du lycée qui rentre,
C'est la tisane sans le foyer,

La phtisie pulmonaire attristant le quartier,
Et toute la misère des grands centres.[37]

The reader has been brought to the position of being
unable to avoid the sudden seriousness of this last line.
Secondly, there is a stiffening of the verbal texture of the
poem, a suddenly distinct picture of the genteel, alien
town, (these are the "objective correlatives" that Eliot
later adopts), the recall of a dominant symbol, (the pianos
heard so often, without intimacy, in the city street), and
the usual compensating irony (what the newspapers have
to report in this little town is the weekly mystery of its
sanitation statistics):

Mais, lainages, caoutchoucs, pharmacie, rêve,
Rideaux écartés du haut des balcons des grèves
Devant l'océan de toitures des faubourgs,
Lampes, estampes, thé, petits-fours,
Serez-vous pas mes seules amours! . . .
(Oh! et puis, est-ce que tu connais, outre les pianos,
Le sobre et vespéral mystère hebdomadaire
Des statistiques sanitaires
Dans les journaux?)[38]

Thirdly, there is the attitude which informs the poem.
In a last line, which is no doubt intentionally ambiguous,
and the seriousness of which is determined by a pun
(coeur/choeur), the poet says that he will try to stay in
tune with the world, and yet simultaneously, in his
capacity as poet, give it its note. The world is nevertheless ridiculous, and only likely to cause anguish whether
one is in tune with it or not. *Le Sanglot de la terre* is re-
presented in this poem by the one phrase, "et la planète
falote," which in turn is immediately balanced by one of
the most delightful lines in any of these poems:

Non, non! c'est la saison et la planète falote!
Que l'autan, que l'autan
Effiloche les savates que le Temps se tricote!

C'est la saison, oh déchirements! c'est la saison!
Tous les ans, tous les ans,
J'essaierai en choeur d'en donner la note.[39]

It is not only because Laforgue's work is hard to obtain
that "L'Hiver qui vient" has been quoted in its entirety.
The *Derniers Vers* are not worth discussing except as whole
poems. A truncated tone-poem is in any case a manifest
absurdity, since it is the interrelationship of the parts, and
the consequent harmony, that is important. Here the
interrelationship has been achieved in a particularly
fine way, it being clear, over and above everything else,
that free-verse as Laforgue wrote it, held firmly by
assonance and rhyme, was as disciplined and controlled
as any other form he might have adopted, yet unobtrusive
as he had always wished. He had made a style.

There are other advantages in being close to the text.
The revised text, as printed here, is from the Mercure de
France edition which was taken verbatim from the
excellent 1890 edition prepared by Dujardin and
Fénéon. Dujardin did not reprint this poem, "L'Hiver
qui vient," as it had appeared in *La Vogue*, since he had
the manuscript which Laforgue had corrected and
emended after the first publication. Some of the changes
are relatively unimportant, others indicate very clearly
the way that his mind was working. The lines:
"D'usines . . . ," "Montant en don quichottesques rails,"
"Pour les soldats loin de la France," "Tous les paniers
Watteau des bourrées sous les marroniers," and "Devant
l'océan de toitures des faubourgs," were not in the *Vogue*
version of the poem as published by Kahn. It can easily
be seen that their inclusion makes the imaginative impact of the poem very much sharper. There was, however,
a change of a different kind, which is much more important. In the earlier version, the last section of the
poem had included the line: "Nul n'en rendra raison"
("There is no reason for it"), which had in turn been

emended in such a way that the poem ended with the
lines "Pour mes compatriotes/Mais qu'on ne m'en
demande pas la raison" ("For my compatriots/But let
no-one ask me the reason for it"). It was just this over-
heavy stress on the futility of existence that made the
earlier poems, particularly *Le Sanglot de la terre*, so
limited. It is therefore interesting to see Laforgue learn-
ing to avoid explicit statement. His attitude to life had
not altered to any great extent, but he now seems to
understand the naïveté of the naked idea, and is in any
case concerned to express, not ideas, but the sum-total of
his imaginative experience, so that his criteria are artistic,
not philosophical, ones.

This evidence of conscious care and craftsmanship can
also be seen in the third of the *Derniers Vers*, "Dimanches,"
though in a different way. Many of the *Derniers Vers* are
based on earlier attempts now gathered together in *Des
fleurs de bonne volonté*. This "Dimanches," for example,
relates back to several of the early poems: "Le vrai de la
chose," "Célibat, célibat," "Gare au bord de le mer,"
and poems XXVIII and XXX in *Des fleurs de bonne
volonté*, which are also called "Dimanches." These early
fragments which contribute to the poem in the *Derniers
Vers* are not poems so much as verbal concoctions round
a single theme or a single experience. Not only are these
experiences seen to have greater significance when they
are absorbed into the substance of the longer poem, but
the play of words is also no longer there for the sake of
the exercise, but now contributes in a pertinent way to
the counterpoint of the tone-poem. Though it is not
possible here to compare these poems in detail, an example will show the kind of change that Laforgue makes.
The "Dimanches" in the *Derniers Vers* begins with the lines:

Bref, j'allais me donner d'un "je vous aime"
Quand je m'avisai non sans peine
Que d'abord je ne me possédais pas bien moi-même.

(Mon Moi, c'est Galathée aveuglant Pygmalion!
Impossible de modifier cette situation.)[40]

Laforgue is thus like the Pre-Raphaelite Pygmalion who
spurns the world, disregards the women of his home
town, dreams of an ideal love, is inspired to create the
ideal form in art, and is rewarded by a statue so perfect
that it comes to life, so that he is after all confronted by
a real Galatea. The irony of this would be very congenial to Laforgue. Since, at more or less the same time,
Laforgue, (in his letter to Kahn of June 1886) was considering an article on Ruskin, and since there are many
references to English painters like Burne-Jones and
Madox-Browne, both in the letters and in *Mélanges
posthumes*, it is tempting to suppose that Laforgue's
interest had increased since his meeting with Leah Lee,
and that he in fact knew of Burne-Jones' four paintings
on the theme of Pygmalion and Galatea. Though there
are other Pre-Raphaelite passages in the *Derniers Vers*
which substantiate his general interest, the precise point
is of course hypothetical. The reference to Pygmalion
has the same effect as the reference to Watteau in
"L'Hiver qui vient": very economically it throws the
first lines into a new perspective. It does this in the same
way as in a painting a tension is produced by the juxta-
position of objects not immediately expected together. It
is also a more than usually oblique way of speaking
about himself, the self-knowledge implied here being
at least more forceful than the open confessions of the
earlier poems. The "Dimanches" of *Des fleurs de bonne
volonté* is at any rate a much cruder piece of work. In it
he plays with a conceit. Marriage is a dancing, colourful
life-buoy; he a morose Corsair, who knows he has been
shipwrecked for ever. Immediately after this, the last
lines of the poem:

Un soir, je crus en Moi! J'en faillis me fiancer!
Est-ce possible . . . Où donc tout ça est-il passé! . . .

Chez moi, c'est Galathée aveuglant Pygmalion!
Ah! faudrait modifier cette situation. . . .)[41]

In the *Derniers Vers* version a good part of the bathos of
this has been omitted, the essential metaphor retained.
In the process it has become quite clear that Laforgue
was aware of the weakness of his distinction between the
Ideal and the Real, though for him it was "Impossible to
alter this situation." "Dimanches" xxviii in *Des fleurs
de bonne volonté* also makes it clear that this same distinction is behind his obsessive interest in Hamlet, since the
epigraph of the poem is Hamlet's conversation with
Ophelia in the play scene. Thus the poem in the *Derniers
Vers* is the expression of the dilemma of the fatalist. Either
he chooses to compromise himself by accepting the world
on terms he knows to be unsatisfactory, or alternatively
he remains aloof without any consolation at all, and
certainly without the satisfaction of believing in his own
judgment.

These examples are not isolated ones. The eighth and
ninth poems in the *Derniers Vers*, for instance, are quite
heavily dependent upon *Des fleurs de bonne volonté*. Draw-
ing upon them at will, he achieves his ideal poem: "a
kind of poetry which would be psychology in the form
of a dream . . . inextricable symphonies with a melodic
phrase, whose curve would reappear from time to time."[42]
This, then, is the last half of the *Derniers Vers*
"Dimanches":

Oh! voilà que ton piano
Me recommence, si natal maintenant!
Et ton coeur qui s'ignore s'y ânonne
En ritournelles de bastringues à tout venant,
Et ta pauvre chair s'y fait mal! . . .
A moi, Walkyries!
Walkyries des hypocondries et des tueries!

Ah! que je te les tordrais avec plaisir,
Ce corps bijou, ce coeur à ténor,

Et te dirais leur fait, et puis encore
La manière de s'en servir
De s'en servir à deux.
Si tu voulais seulement m'approfondir ensuite un peu!

Non, non! C'est sucer la chair d'un coeur élu,
Adorer d'incurables organes
S'entrevoir avant que les tissus se fanent
En monomanes, en reclus!

Et ce n'est pas sa chair qui me serait tout.
Et je ne serais pas qu'un grand coeur pour elle,
Mais quoi s'en aller faire les fous
Dans des histoires fraternelles!

L'âme et la chair, la chair et l'âme,
C'est l'esprit édénique et fier
D'être un peu l'Homme avec la Femme.

En attendant, oh! garde-toi des coups de tête,
Oh! file ton rouet et prie et reste honnête.

—Allons, dernier des poètes,
Toujours enfermé tu te rendras malade!
Vois, il fait beau temps, tout le monde est dehors,
Va donc acheter deux sous d'ellébore,
Ça te fera une petite promenade.[43]

Again there is the balance or counterpoint of the last
lines, anticipating, for example, passages in Joyce. Disgust is weighed against charity, then dissolved into a
final irony. He will tolerate neither a bluntly sexual union
nor an anaemic brotherly affair, a Platonic friendship.
Rather he will go for a little walk: "Go out and buy a
pennyworth of hellebore." This hellebore, with its highly
pertinent and delightful reference back to the tortoise
and the hare of Lafontaine, is both the "realist's" laxa-
tive that will purge the poet of the neuroticism of the

poem and the "classical" remedy for madness. The irony that was at an earlier date contained in violent and shocking contrasts is now achieved economically with the pointing of a single word.

The verbal felicity of this ending adds to, but of course does not replace, Laforgue's customary exuberance. Indeed the very next poem begins with a vigorous verbal picture of autumn, where the effect is visual but is achieved by a rapid association of ideas: the autumn wind and the closing down of everything for the winter bring to the poet's mind a rapid succession of images. The play on the word "feuille" and the inclusion of "des Antigones, des Philomèles," which though the names of plays carry the weight of classical allusion, might be a little distasteful if given emphasis. But the passage is too energetic and varied for that:

> C'est l'automne, l'automne, l'automne,
> Le grand vent et toute sa séquelle
> De représailles! et de musiques! . . .
> Rideaux tirés, clôture annuelle,
> Chute des feuilles, des Antigones, des Philomèles:
> Mon fossoyeur, *Alas poor Yorick!*
> Les remue à la pelle! . . .
>
> Vivent l'Amour et les feux de paille! . . .
>
> Les Jeunes Filles inviolables et frêles
> Descendent vers la petite chapelle
> Dont les chimériques cloches
> Du joli, joli dimanche
> Hygiéniquement et élégamment les appellent.[44]

It is this fourth poem in the *Derniers Vers* (and the second "Dimanches") that laments the fate of the genteel girl, the Ophelia, who is forced to live life as it is and even to believe in her religious upbringing. The debate about this is ended in a particularly blunt way. Mass, and the social

H

parade or *bourgeois* ritual in the hour after High Mass each Sunday, were Laforgue's symbols of futility, of the unthinking, automatic existence that he felt most people lead. "Might we leave this life together, after Mass," he says, "nauseated by our species that yawns, replete, at the church steps." But the French is more neat and therefore more telling:

> Oh! puissions-nous quitter la vie
> Ensemble dès cette Grand'Messe,
> Ecoeurés de notre espèce
> Qui baille assouvie
> Dès le parvis! . . .[45]

There is no doubt about the ferocity of this feeling in Laforgue. His distrust of life is complete. In the next poem, "Pétition," there is the image of "la divine Rosace," the west window of the Cathedral, which was the conventional symbol for Justice and which Laforgue remembered nostalgically from his Paris days. What was made a whole poem in *Le Sanglot de la terre* ("Devant la grande rosace en vitraille de Notre-Dame"),[46] is integrated into the *Derniers Vers*. The window, like the bouquet of orange blossom, carried by a bride and set in satin, sees only marriages of sex, delivered in bulk to run trippingly to a common grave.

> O bouquets d'oranger cuirassés de satin,
> Elle s'éteint, elle s'éteint,
> La divine Rosace
> A voir vos noces de sexes livrés à la grosse
> Courir en valsant vers la fosse
> Commune! . . . Pauvre race!
>
> Pas d'absolu; des compromis;
> Tout est pas plus, tout est permis.[47]

On the other hand, although this antipathy and distrust remain dominant, another theme runs through the poems which is more sympathetic, charitable and hopeful. In this poem, while most women are "slaves," and have been throughout history, he wishes her to stop thinking about ideals and chimerical mysteries, to be content simply with human relationships: "If she would only accept man as an equal."[48] The mild humanism suggested by lines like these is of course entirely in keeping both with his pessimistic atitude to life and with his view of art as being concerned with everyday affairs rather than with hypothetical moral values and ideals. The determinist who does not believe in another world is obliged to make the best of the one he has; and, though Laforgue is not very concerned with theories, he had said—when obliged to think about the subject— that the arts develop a man's sensibility to the full, and therefore give him the greatest possible chance of understanding the life that he has to lead.[49] In the very next poem, "Simple Agonie," he says that, with the world as it is, "I shall make for myself a more human world!" He describes a part of his decadent life:

> J'entasse sur mon lit, les journaux, linge sale,
> Dessins de mode, photographies quelconques,
> Toute la capitale,
> Matrice sociale, . . .[50]

and wishes to break with it: "There's only one thing to do:/Smash everything." But it is said to be too late for this, so the poet, who at the beginning of the poem had the ambition at least—with his unique melody—to tell "la chose qu'est la chose," ends only with the satisfaction of not having compromised himself. He will no longer be seen on national holidays enclosing and bolting himself into history, for though he came too soon to the world to do as he wished, at least he left without doing anything scandalous, which is the most that anyone could do. "O you who are listening to me, return each one of you to your homes."[51]

This line of thought, or *leit-motif*, never so much as approaches optimism, but the humanity which it implies certainly relieves the general atmosphere, so that there is nothing in Laforgue as morbid as in many of Hardy's poems. In the second half of the *Derniers Vers* this humanity is expressed in a more personal way. The two lovers of the poems are like the lovers he sees by the roadside, who gesticulate outside the law, and though, as the years pass, each person for himself has to learn to grow hard, the poet cannot prevent the feeling of a real compassion for the other person which runs parallel to the self-pity that he feels for himself:

> Seul sous les vieux cieux
> De me faire le fou
> Le fou sans feux ni lieux.[52]

She, who "is not like the others," should not abandon herself to these wretched games, so that if she does her best to stay as good as gold he will try to love "the past that lies behind the beautiful eyes—the eyes of an orphan heroine."[53] In other words, the poet who three years before was at pains to remind his friends that he had "sojourned in the Cosmos" is now content with something more human, more compassionate, and perhaps more real. There may be readers who find biographical explanations for this. Laforgue had met Leah Lee in January, had almost become engaged in the spring, was away from Berlin during the summer while he was writing the poems, and may very well have regretted the continuation of his dilettante life, as well as the lost opportunity. But if such an explanation were possible, it would of course not affect the meaning or the quality of the poems.

What would affect the quality of the poems would be lack of control in the handling of the more personal themes. In "Solo de lune," this control is reasserted. From the beginning Laforgue has been writing a poem on the musical analogy, trying to create with words the "pure" art of music. On one level there have been innumerable specific reminders: the chorus of the first poem, the three horns of the second, the "Walkyries du vent" of the third, the theatre music of the fourth, the tambourines and trumpets of the fifth, and finally:

> Ma mélodie, toute et unique, monte,
> Dans le soir et redouble, et fasse tout ce qu'elle peut
> Et dise le chose qu'est la chose,
> Et retombe, et reprenne,
> Et fasse de la peine,
> O solo de sanglots.[54]

On another level he does in French what Hopkins at more or less the same time did in English: produces musical effects of considerable variety with the tonal qualities of words, so that the sense of the poem literally reaches the reader through the sound, or if not that way, then hardly at all. The point of writing free-verse, therefore, is not merely that it permits a greater naturalness of expression by letting the poet concentrate on the "thing itself," but also that a greater wealth of musical possibility becomes available to the poet, so that it is feasible after all to write a poem in which to distinguish between sound and sense is impossible since both are absorbed in the same art.

There is one further point to discuss. Several of the *Derniers Vers* are in the form of a dialogue. Whereas in the discussion so far it has sometimes been difficult to distinguish between the poet and the "character" of a poem, in these particular poems, (for example VIII and IX,) there is the device of a debate or conversation between man and woman, with the poet as third party. So the first part of "Légende" is a confession on the part of the girl, ribbed with ironical details, as though the love she confessed belonged to another age altogether. The second part is the conversation of the lovers themselves, against a similar mock-romantic tableau. Only after the presentation of these two insubstantial pieces does one get the perspective of the poem. These things to the poet are the legends of the golden age, with which on the mundane level he might very well have competed, though not with total seriousness as the irony of the last lines shows:

> Moi qui lui eusse été dans tout l'art des Adams
> Des Edens aussi hyperboliquement fidèle
> Que l'est le Soleil chaque soir envers l'Occident! . . .[55]

In the ninth poem, which has already been mentioned, it is only the woman who speaks with a series of short statements, as though answering, as in Browning, the objections of a companion who remains grimly silent. She proposes to take the romantic risk of believing in life without reason. He does not answer, but ends with the cynical but rather effective lines:

> Ainsi, elle viendrait, évadée, demi-morte,
> Se rouler sur le paillasson que j'ai mis à cet effet devant ma porte
> Ainsi, elle viendrait à Moi avec des yeux absolument fous,
> Et elle me suivrait avec ses yeux-là partout, partout![56]

It is at this point that comparison is often made with Eliot, who succeeds in absorbing this kind of dramatic element into his early poems, so that it is an organic part of the poem, whereas Laforgue is really only writing the same kind of poem as elsewhere in the *Derniers Vers*, but from a different point of view. Eliot succeeds in this because he makes the imagined character more distinct and visible, and because the dramatic situation is more self-contained, and apparently at a distance from the mind of the poet. It is only an apparent distance, however, for the greater the artifice the more exactly does the mask reveal the essential features beneath. Laforgue does not do this. It was not this kind of art he desired. On the contrary, he lived precariously at the boundary line between belief and knowledge: he wished to believe, but thought that the world made this impossible; and the poems express the contradictions of this, with a wry irony, a degree of bitterness, and considerable emotional energy.

These qualities are seen, finally, in the concluding lines of the last of the *Derniers Vers*, perhaps the last lines of poetry that Laforgue wrote. The issue of the poem as a whole has not been resolved, since he still feels that freedom is imaginary, or a matter of biological necessity, and that behind the beautiful eyes of the woman there is a Jung-like past which he should know better than to accept. But as has been seen, he has also become aware of the weakness of his own position, and at the same time come to feel a degree of sympathy, if not love, which has obliged him to exchange his total cynicism for something very much more tentative:

La nuit est à jamais noire,
Le vent est grandement triste,
Tout dit la vieille histoire
Qu'il faut être deux au coin du feu,

Tout bâcle un hymne fataliste,
Mais toi, il ne faut pas que tu t'abandonnes,
A ces vilains jeux! . . .

A ces grandes pitiés du mois de novembre!
Reste dans ta petite chambre,
Passe, à jamais glacée,
Tes beaux yeux irréconciliablement baissés.

Oh! qu'elle est là-bas, que la nuit est noire!
Que la vie est une étourdissante foire!
Que toutes sont créature, et que tout est routine!

Oh! que nous mourrons!

> Eh bien, pour aimer ce qu'il y a d'histoires
> Derrière ces beaux yeux d'orpheline héroïne,
> O Nature, donne-moi la force et la courage
> De me croire en âge,
> O Nature, relève-moi le front!
> Puisque, tôt ou tard, nous mourrons. . . .[57]

If one considers the *Derniers Vers* as a whole, it can be seen that they demonstrate only too well one of the principal dilemmas of the modern poet. From this time on, it is as though the poet has the option of writing a poem which satisfies his feeling for art or of remaining close to life as he knows it even if that entails writing a more limited kind of poem. Valéry did the first, Apollinaire the second. The "romantic" position that Laforgue was in had become untenable. After this, it could not, by any stretch of the imagination, be claimed that the view of a single man, that is, his thoughts and impressions as opposed to anyone else's, were of central importance, so that if a poet wished to say anything of importance on a level not his own, he had to that extent to sacrifice his own particular, arbitrary kaleidoscope of experience. This is what Laforgue wryly anticipates when he says: "I've not done things well."[58] His decadence is the result of his understanding that his thinking life did not "rhyme" with anything real in the universe, where "the stars are more numerous than grains of sand." And it is the very "upbringing" here lamented by Laforgue that a few years later Eliot firmly rejects, first by following through Laforgue's development from beginning to end (so that "Prufrock" is the exact parallel to the *Derniers Vers*); then by taking the artistic implications of that development one step further, in *The Waste Land*; then by recognising the limitations of that still "romantic" poem and following his own insight to the *Four Quartets*. So Eliot avoids the incipient neuroticism of "The Love Song of J. Alfred Prufrock," which is Laforgue's decadence, not by the skills of irony, understatement, drama, and free-verse, which he partly learns from Laforgue, and which are the concomitant and necessary features of poems like "The Love Song of J. Alfred Prufrock" and the *Derniers Vers*, but by positively avoiding the predicament in which that kind of mask was necessary. Though Eliot's interest in Laforgue (from the time he purchased the 1902 edition in Boston after his return from Europe) is, on the evidence of his work, not to be doubted, these remarks are not aimed at establishing an influence, an exercise which in most cases is completely unimportant and arbitrary, but at defining one of the positions that a twentieth-century poet might be in. It is one of several possibilities. Wallace Stevens, for example, starts from the same position as Laforgue was in. He occupies himself with the same philosophical difficulties, is trapped almost by the acute determinism of his own epistemology, and spends his writing life trying to write a poem which will be faithful both to his own feelings and the world as he knows it. His compromise, however, is not as ruthless as Eliot's. He adopts a tentative humanism, (an expedient, though without the bitterness of Laforgue) and by doing so accepts the limitations that this imposes on him as poet. Laforgue, from this point of view, has the importance of a geologist who has explored a certain area, "mon Afrique intérieure," as he said earlier; perhaps a geologist of some standing, since he also provided the people who came after him with the means by which they might make the same exploration, and indeed go further. Specifically, he showed that it was possible to write a free-verse poem, of great musicality, where the imaginative discipline was at the very heart of the poem, and not a matter of externals; he found a way of using symbol as the direct expression of the poet's insight; and, by dint of sheer virtuosity, he moved poetry into the realm of art, in the twentieth-century sense, and away from the romantic context of moral communication.

Laforgue's contribution to the craft of poetry is there-fore considerable, whereas the Pre-Raphaelites, in rather a similar position, because of their preoccupation with the past had missed the opportunity of making significant technical progress. He created a new poetic idiom simply by writing it. As a person, he represents the disengaged, *fin-de-siècle*, self-conscious mind, at odds with the world yet obliged to place trust in his own untrusting sensibility. In this he was not alone. Nor is it likely that he would change his attitude today.

REFERENCES

1. *O.C.*, v. 147–8.
2. *L.A.*, p. 163.
3. *O.C.*, v. 148.
4. *L.A.*, p. 217.
5. *O.C.*, v. 156.
6. *L.A.*, pp. 220–1.
7. *O.C.*, v. 162.
8. *O.C.*, v. 165.
9. *O.C.*, v. 171.
10. *O.C.*, v. 171.
11. *O.C.*, v. 191.
12. *Poésies complètes*, Paris 1894.
13. *L.A.*, XLIV.
14. *O.C.*, II. 151.
15. *O.C.*, II. 152.
16. *O.C.*, II. 153.
17. *O.C.*, II. 158.
18. *O.C.*, II. 156. "I have travelled by floes of ice more pure than first com-municants in white. . . . I do not go to church not I! I'm the High Chancellor of Analysis, in fact. Just bear that in mind."
19. *O.C.*, II. 159.
20. *O.C.*, II. 160.
21. *O.C.*, II. 163.
22. *O.C.*, II. 167.
23. *O.C.*, II. 170.
24. *O.C.*, II. 170.
25. *O.C.*, II. 172. "I would have been the model husband! As the swish of your dress is the model of sound."
26. *O.C.*, II. 174.
27. *O.C.*, II. 182.
28. *O.C.*, II. 186. "I would be no more than a last resort, as are indeed my day in Time and my place in Space. No-one could wish me to accommodate my-self to this completely disgusting fate!"
29. *O.C.*, II. 189. "In my home town, which has barely twenty thousand souls, there is a nunnery facing the cathedral, between the police station and the school."
30. *O.C.*, II. 191.
31. *O.C.*, II. 191. "O Nature, give me strength and courage to think myself of

age. O Nature, lift up my head, for sooner or later we shall die. . . ."

32. *O.C.*, II. 143. "Sentimental blockade! Packets from the Levant! Oh, falling rain! Oh, falling dusk! Oh, the wind! . . . All Saints' Day, Christmas Day, and New Year's Eve, oh! in the drizzle, all my factory chimneys. . . ."

33. "No more sitting, all the benches are wet; it's all quite finished, believe me, until next year. All the benches are wet, so rusted are the woods, such a call have the horns made, such a sounding call! . . . Ah! clouds hustling in from the channel shore, you have spoilt for us our last week-end."

34. "It's drizzling; in the rain-drenched forest, the spider-webs give beneath the water-drops: it is their downfall. Suns, Surveyors of Work at the gold-mines of Pactolus, at agricultural shows, where are you buried? This evening a spent sun lies flat out on the hill-top—lies on his side, in the broom, on his cloak, a sun as white as the spittle in a tavern lying on a litter of yellow broom, the yellow broom of autumn. And the horns call out to him: 'Come back. . . . Come back to life! Tally-ho! Tally-ho! and in at the death!" O

sad dirge, have you finished! And they fool about while he lies there, like a torn gland in the neck, and he shivers, without anyone! . . ."

35. "Forward, forward, and away! It's good old winter back again. Oh, the winding high-roads with no Little Red Riding Hood making her way there! . . . Oh, the ruts they have from last month's carts, rising like Don Quixotic rails towards the retreating cloud patrols that the wind now harries to transatlantic folds! . . . Faster, faster, it's the season itself, this time, and the wind, this night, has made fine work of it! O havoc! O nests, O genteel little gardens! My heart and my slumber: O the echoing axes! . . ."

36. "All these boughs still had their green leaves; now the dead leaves moulder beneath them. Leaves, little leaves, may a brave wind carry you in long trails to the ponds, or the game-keepers' fires, or the pallets of ambulances for soldiers far from France. It's the season, the season, the sledge-hammers are invaded by rust; the telegraph wires in their kilometric spleen are gnawed by rust on the high-roads where nobody goes. The horns, the horns,

the horns—melancholy
horns!... They've gone
away, changing their tone,
changing their music and
their tone, Halloo, Halloo,
Hall-ay! The horns, the
horns, the horns, have on
the north wind gone
away. I can't abandon
this note: such echoes it
has!..."

37. "It's the season, the season,
the harvest is done! Here
come the rains with the
patience of a saint. Fare-
well the harvests, and fare-
well all the baskets and
hoops of the Watteau
dances under the chestnut
trees. It's the dormitory
coughing of schools at the
new term; it's the herb-
tea away from home, the
tubercular affliction of the
district, and the whole
misery of the city centre."

38. "But woollens, goloshes, the
chemist's, dream, balcony
curtains drawn back on
the high shore by the
ocean of suburban roofs—
lamps, prints, tea, petits-
fours, will you not be my
only loves!... Oh! and
then, quite apart from the
pianos, do you know the
restrained, the weekly,
the vesperal mystery of
sanitation statistics in the
Press?"

39. "No, no! it's the season, and
the planet's grotesque!
May the gales from the
south unravel the slippers
Time knits for himself!

It's the season, oh an-
guish, the season! Every
year, every year, I will
try as in chorus to give it
its tone."

40. *O.C.*, ii. 151. "In short, I
was going to treat my-
self to an 'I love you'
when I realised, but not
without trouble, that in
the first place I was not
really in possession of
myself. (Galatea blinding
Pygmalion—that's my
Self. Impossible to alter
this situation.)"

41. *O.C.*, ii. 66. "One night, I
believed in my Self! I
very nearly became en-
gaged! Is it possible...
where has it all gone!...
With me, its Galatea
blinding Pygmalion! Ah!
this situation should be
altered...."

42. *O.C.*, iv. 66.

43. *O.C.*, ii. 153. "Oh! and now
your piano sets me going
agin, like a new birth!
And your heart, not
knowing itself, stammers
out dance hall tunes to all
who come, and your poor
flesh is hurt! Come to me,
Walkyries of hypochon-
dria and slaughter! Oh,
with what pleasure I'd
wring them, this precious
body and this tenor heart,
and I'd tell you their
point, and then again the
way for us both to use
them. If afterwards you
would only probe me a
little more deeply! No, no!

That's to suck the flesh of a chosen spirit, to adore incurable organs, to glimpse one another before the tissues wither into monomaniacs, into hermits. And it's not her flesh that would be everything for me. And for her I'd be more than a large-hearted man. But what's the point of making a fool of oneself with talk of brotherly love! The spirit and the flesh, the flesh and the spirit—it is the proud spirit of the Garden of Eden to be something of a Man with Woman. Meanwhile, keep yourself from rash action; oh! spin your wheel and pray and remain virtuous.—Come, last of poets, if you're always shut up, you will make yourself ill. See, it's a fine day, everyone's outside. Then go and buy a pennyworth of hellebore. It will give you a little walk."

44. *O.C.*, II. 155. "It's autumn, autumn, autumn, the high wind and its whole train of reprisals and music. Curtains drawn, the seasons' end, the fall of leaves, of Antigones, of Philomelas; my grave-digger, *Alas poor Yorick!* disturbs them with his spade! Three cheers for Love and short-lived flames! Young ladies, frail, inviolate, walk down to

their little church, called by their darling Sunday bells, called by chimerical bells with an antiseptic elegance."

45. *O.C.*, II. 158.

46. *O.C.*, I. 48.

47. *O.C.*, II. 159. "Bouquets of orange blossom with satin armour-plating—the divine rose-window grows faint at the sight of your sex-weddings delivered in bulk and rapidly dancing away to a common grave!... Poor race! There are no absolutes, only compromise; everything is at a minimum, anything goes."

48. *O.C.*, II. 161.

49. *M.P.*, p. 205.

50. *O.C.*, II. 164. "On my bed I pile up dirty clothes, newspapers, fashion designs, ordinary photographs, the entire capital, the womb of society."

51. *O.C.*, II. 166.

52. *O.C.*, II. 182. "I make a fool of myself, alone beneath the antique skies, a poor fool without hearth or home."

53. *O.C.*, II. 191.

54. *O.C.*, II. 163. "In the evening my melody, whole and unique, rises, and falls, and does all that it can, and tells the thing as it is, and falls again, and rises, and is the cause of grief, a solo of weeping."

55. *O.C.*, II. 176. "I who, with an art like that of Adam in Paradise, would have

been as hyperbolically faithful to her as the sun is, each evening, to the western horizon."

56. *O.C.*, II. 179. "And so, having escaped, she would come, half-dead, and fling herself on the mat I've placed by my door for that very purpose; and so she would come to me with utterly wild eyes, and those eyes would follow me everywhere, everywhere!"

57. *O.C.*, II. 190–91. "The night is forever dark, the wind extremely sad. Everything repeats the same old tale: one has to be two in the chimney nook. Everything bungles a fatalistic hymn; but you, you must not abandon yourself to these scurvy tricks!... to these great pities of November! Stay in your little chambers and pass by, forever frigid, your lovely eyes uncompromisingly downcast.—Oh, how far away she is, how dark the night! What a deafening fairground is life! Frailty thy name is woman—and everything routine. Oh!... we shall die! To love what there is of knowledge behind the lovely eyes of this orphan heroine, O Nature, give me strength and courage to think myself of age; O Nature, lift up my head, for sooner or later we shall die...."

58. *O.C.*, II. 169.

SELECT BIBLIOGRAPHY

I. LAFORGUE

1. Verse

Les Complaintes. Paris (Vanier) 1885.
L'Imitation de Notre Dame la Lune. Paris (Vanier) 1886.
Le Concile féerique. Paris, Publications de la Vogue, 1886.
Les Derniers Vers de Jules Laforgue. Tours (Deslis) 1890.
Poésies Complètes. Paris (Vanier) 1894.

2. Prose

Moralités légendaires. Paris (Librairie de la Revue Indépendante) 1887.
Lettres à un ami. 1880–86. Paris (Mercure de France) 1941.
Stéphane Vassiliew. Geneva (P. Cailler) 1946.

3. Miscellaneous

Walt Whitman. Oeuvres choisies. Paris (Editions N.R.F.) 1918.

4. Collected Works

Oeuvres complètes de Jules Laforgue. 4 vols. Paris (Mercure de France) 1902–3: Vol. I, *Moralités légendaires*; Vol. II and Vol. III, *Poésies*; Vol. IV, *Mélanges posthumes*.
Editions de la Connaissance. 3 vols. Paris 1920–21: Vol. I, *Chroniques parisiennes*; Vol. II, *Dragées. Charles Baudelaire. Tristan Corbière*; Vol. III, *Exil. Poésie. Spleen*.
Oeuvres complètes de Jules Laforgue. 6 vols. Paris (Mercure de France) 1920–30; Vols. I and II, *Poésies*; Vol. III, *Moralités légendaires*; Vols. IV and V, *Lettres*; Vol. VI, *En Allemagne. Berlin, la cour et la ville. Une vengeance à Berlin*. This volume also includes the *Agenda* for 1883.
Les Complaintes. L'Imitation de Notre Dame la Lune. Derniers Vers. Paris (Librairie Armand Colin) 1959.

II. OTHERS

BOLGAR, R. R.: "The Present State of Laforgue Studies," in *French Studies*, IV, Jul. 1950.
CUISINIER, J.: *Jules Laforgue*. Paris 1925.
DUFOUR, M.: *Etude sur l'Esthétique de J. Laforgue*. Paris 1904.
DUJARDIN, E.: "Les Premiers Poètes du Vers Libre," in *Mercure de France*, March 1921.

Durry, Marie-Jeanne: *Jules Laforgue*. Paris, 1952.

Fargue, L. P.: "Jules Laforgue," in *Revue de Paris*, Apr. 1935.

Greene, E. J. H.: *T. S. Eliot et la France*. Bouvin 1951.

——: "Jules Laforgue et T. S. Eliot," in *Revue de littérature comparée*, 22ᵉ année (Jul.–Sep. 1948) pp. 363–97.

Guichard, Leon: *Jules Laforgue et ses poésies*. Grenoble 1950.

Hays, H. R.: "Laforgue and Wallace Stevens," in *Romanic Review*, xxv, 1934, pp. 242–8.

Kahn Gustave: *Symbolistes et décadents.* 902.

——: "J. es Laforgue," in *Les L.* vi No. 298. Paris (Vanier) 886

——: "Jules

Mauclair, C.: *Essai sur Jules Laforgue*. Paris 1896.

Moimandre, Francis de: "Jules Laforgue," in *Mercure de France*, xlv (1903), pp. 289–314.

Pound, Ezra: "Irony, Laforgue and Some Satire," printed in *Literary Essays of Ezra Pound*. London 1960.

—— : "A study of French Poets," reprinted in *Ma* 935, pp. 159–247.

nnel, Peter: *Baudelaire and the Symbolists*. London 1929.

sey, Warren: *Laforgue and the Ironic Inheritance.* 1953.

oul, Pierre: *Laforgue*. Paris 1960.

gnier, H. de: *Faces et Profiles. Souvenirs sur Villiers de l'Is* am, *Jules Laforgue, Stéphane Mallarmé*. Paris 1931.

Ruchon, François: *Laforgue, sa vie, son oeuvre*. Geneva 1929.

Symons, Arthur: "The Decadent Movement in Literature" in *Harper's New Monthly Magazine*, lxxxvii (Nov. 189 pp. 858–67.

——: *The Symbolist Movement in Literature*. London 1899.

Turnell, Martin: "Jules Laforgue," in *Scrutiny*, v (1939).

——: "Jules Laforgue," in *Cornhill Magazine*, London, 973 (Winter 1947–8) pp. 74–90.